FEARLESS & FREE

Also by Victoria Osteen

Exceptional You!

Exceptional You! Study Guide

Exceptional You Journal

Love Your Life

Daily Readings from Love Your Life

Unexpected Treasures

Gifts from the Heart

My Happy Heart Books

Wake Up to Hope (with Joel Osteen)

Our Best Life Together (with Joel Osteen)

FEARLESS & FREE

INSPIRATIONAL THOUGHTS TO SET YOUR ATTITUDE AND ACTIONS FOR A GREAT DAY!

VICTORIA OSTEEN

Faith Words

New York • Nashville

FaithWords
Hachette Book Group
1290 Avenue of the Americas, New York, NY 10104
faithwords.com
twitter.com/faithwords

First edition: April 2020

FaithWords is a division of Hachette Book Group, Inc. The FaithWords name and logo are trademarks of Hachette Book Group, Inc.

The publisher is not responsible for websites (or their content) that are not owned by the publisher.

The Hachette Speakers Bureau provides a wide range of authors for speaking events. To find out more, go to www.hachettespeakersbureau.com or call (866) 376-6591.

Print book interior by Bart Dawson

Library of Congress Control Number: 2020932459

ISBN: 978-1-5460-1070-8 (hardcover), 978-1-5460-1796-7 (large print), 978-1-5460-1756-1 (special edition), 978-1-5460-1067-8 (ebook)

Printed in the United States of America

LSC-C

10 9 8 7 6 5 4 3 2 1

Contents

· · · · · ● ● ● · · · · ·

To every person who is on their journey

to live fearlessly in the truth that God

has already set them free

Introduction

· · · · · ● ● ● · · · ·

What does it take to live a life that is fearless and free? Is it even possible in these frantic times when the demands of our lives are in a constant state of acceleration? God promises us that living a life of fearlessness and freedom is not only possible but a natural outflow of the interaction between His goodness and grace and our attitudes and actions. Choosing to believe this promise is the first very important step to living the life you want to live.

Your thoughts, attitudes, and actions have incredible power in your life. Are you embracing the promises of God during the season you're living in? Do you have an attitude of abundance and of gratitude for God's grace and goodness? Are you being intentional with your time? Are you being faithful with the small stuff? Are you storing up God's Word? Are you committed to love? Are you delighting in God? With the go-go-go of daily life, it's so important you ask yourself questions like these so you can stay grounded in the gifts with which God has graced you. Take a moment to refresh your perspective, because God has already given you everything you need to live fearlessly and freely.

Think about the lives of many people in the Bible. Esther was a young Jewish orphan living in exile in Persia. Her future would, by its very nature and circumstances, be extremely difficult. Like other young girls in her position, there was little promise for a full, happy life. But through her trials, she always believed in the promises of God and what they meant for her—uniquely and personally. For years, she remembered the words of faith and hope she received from her cousin Mordecai. Mordecai would look at Esther and say, "You have what it takes. You were put on this earth to do great things and your life is meant to make a difference." Those words stuck with her and shaped her thoughts. Esther was able to believe in and become the champion God made her to be. She embraced a life of victory, and Mordecai's encouragement helped her recognize her value and potential.

Nehemiah also lived in exile in Persia and was the cupbearer of another king. When he heard that the walls of Jerusalem remained broken down, he had a desire to go and rebuild, but he had no resources, no money, no expertise, and no influence. He wasn't a cabinet member or a general or even a builder. But he prayed and prayed. He asked for God's help and through his faith in God's promises, the king not only granted Nehemiah's request but sent with him the resources and the official papers to do the work. Still, people from various lands who had settled near Jerusalem resisted Nehemiah's work. Nehemiah persevered through strong opposition, suffering, and discouragement, and God sustained him as the walls of Jerusalem were rebuilt.

Joshua and Caleb, two among the Israelites God delivered from Egypt, were tasked with scouting the unknown Promised Land and determining what their people would face when they tried to enter. They saw beyond the obstacles of walled cities and fearsome giants; they saw an opportunity for God to work in their lives, for God to provide for them. They saw an opportunity to possess a promise and let God fight their battles for them. When the other spies came back and warned everyone that the giants were too big to be overcome, Joshua and Caleb believed, and declared, otherwise. Their positive attitudes and their faith allowed them to see what the other leaders were blind to. While everyone else was paralyzed by fear, Joshua and Caleb saw the goodness of God in front of them.

When you open this book and read these words, I want you to be encouraged. I want you to realize that you are already equipped to overcome your fears and limitations. You are already like Esther, with the ability to love yourself and store up God's word, never forgetting that your ordinary is extraordinary. You are already like Nehemiah, as you stay determined, do good work, and dedicate your actions to God, spreading His message by example. You are already like Joshua and Caleb when you refuse to give life to that negativity while keeping your attitude positive and bright.

I want you to feel encouraged each day to love your routine. I want you to feel fully capable of pressing on through the fearful moments you face and reaching your highest potential. And just as I hope these things for you, God has orchestrated your life to accomplish it all. With each of the entries in this book, it is my prayer that you will be filled with confidence that you have what you need to become fearless and free. God has equipped you to push through your fears and become all that He created you to be and have all that He created for you to have.

When Joel and I took over as pastors of Lakewood Church, I had to confront so many of my fears—primarily, my fear of public speaking. Up until then, I didn't have much experience talking in front of large groups of people. The entire week leading up to each service, I would be filled with anxiety, doubt, and dread. How was I supposed to do this every Sunday? I felt those thoughts of defeat swirling in my head. But then, I came to the realization the feelings I felt were all just symptoms of fear.

However, fear was only part of the problem. Not only did I have to recognize that I was living in fear, but I also had to realize that God had already planted seeds in me, seeds that would enable me to do what I needed to do. Everything I needed was already there; I just had to nourish the seeds and allow them to sprout and give me confidence to rise. When I connected with this truth, it allowed me to confront my fears, and I was able to step into all that God had arranged for me.

I have discovered that when I incorporate the following

truths and practices into my life, I begin to see myself as God sees me—as free and strong and confident. Whatever you're facing, I believe that God wants to do the same thing in your life. Be encouraged today because there is so much more in you that is waiting to be discovered. You'll be amazed at the impact these truths will have when you tap into them and believe in the champion God made you to be. My hope is that you trust in God's hands, that you are not stopped by fear, that you grow in joy, and that you live in the freedom to enjoy each day.

I believe this book will be a blessing to you and that it will help you become more aware of the goodness in your life. I want you to feel rejuvenated and excited every morning when you wake up. As you acknowledge your own ability to control your thoughts, attitudes, and actions, you will live fearlessly and freely, just as God intended.

One

· · · · · ● ● ● · · · ·

God's Unconditional Love

See what great love the Father has lavished on us,
that we should be called children of God.

1 JOHN 3:1 NIV

When we were children, the way to win the approval of others was to be on our best behavior. If we were good and behaved appropriately, then we were allowed to go outside and play with our friends. If we acted up and didn't do the right thing, then our privileges were taken away.

Parents and those who teach us have a responsibility to foster good character in us; rewarding or withholding privileges is just one of many ways they might give instruction about what's right and what's wrong. The way we perceive that discipline can feel like rejection or acceptance. Those childhood experiences can affect the way we view God's attitude toward us as adults. Many times we think God is up in Heaven keeping a scorecard, counting our mistakes against us. We wonder what our rating is today. *Is God mad at us or are we on His good side?*

Those thoughts couldn't be further from the truth. God is not deciding whether He loves and accepts us based on our actions. His love for us is unchanging and unconditional. If God's love or approval for us were based on our actions that would be conditional love. John 3:16 says that God so loved the world He gave His only Son for us…unconditionally. He loved us and approved us before we could do right or wrong. He knew us and approved us before we were born. We can't work enough or be good enough to earn God's love and approval; we can only believe and receive it.

If we are going to live fearlessly and free, we need to let go of the idea that God is keeping score. Otherwise, we will struggle throughout our lives, feeling guilty and condemned by our mistakes. I've talked to people who feel like they could never measure up to God's standards, so they don't even try. They don't believe God will listen to them, so they don't pray and ask God to help them.

For I am convinced that neither death nor life, neither angels nor demons, neither the present nor the future, nor any powers, neither height nor depth, nor anything else in all creation, will be able to separate us from the love of God that is in Christ Jesus our Lord.

—ROMANS 8:38–39 NIV

If you feel like that today, I encourage you to shake off that mind-set and open your heart to receive the unconditional love God has freely given you. God knows every mistake that you will ever make. All of your days have been written in His book, from the beginning to the end. God knows every time you'll fail, take the easy way out, or lose your temper, and the good news is, God still chooses you. He still says, "That's my child," and He'll still help you fulfill your destiny. Why? Because God's love is not based on your performance.

Knowing that God loves you unconditionally, you can live free from condemnation and negative self-talk. Certainly, you should try each day to honor God, but don't beat yourself up if you don't perform perfectly all the time. God loves you the way you are, so get up in the morning and say, "Lord, I'm going to be my very best today, knowing that I'm not perfect but that You are, and trusting that there's nothing You won't help me overcome." If you build your life on this foundational truth—that God loves you deeply and unconditionally—then you can live strong and steady. You won't be focused on works, trying to be good enough to be loved by your Heavenly Father. You won't exhaust yourself trying to convince God that you're worthy of His love.

You never want to fall into the trap of trying to convince God how good you've been lately. Justifying why He should bless you, basing His love on your good works. That kind of thinking causes us to shift our perspective and start judging who is and is not worthy of God's love. And, can I tell you something? None of us is worthy. You can't work for God's love; you can only receive it. The work has been done. The price has been paid. You could never pay the price that Jesus paid. He has already stamped the bill "Paid in full." And because of that, you are loved unconditionally and can walk freely in His grace and mercy.

. . . .

Heavenly Father,

Thank You for demonstrating Your love for me through Jesus, Who covered my faults with grace, giving me hope and a future in You. There is no way that I could have earned Your approval, but I'm so thankful that You chose to love me unconditionally anyway. I accept the gift of Christ, and I praise You for what that means to me and for loving me even when I make mistakes. Thank You for giving me the desire to please You and to get better every day—not to earn Your love, but so that I can live my life free to love You, and to love others the same way You love me.

In Jesus' name,
Amen

· · · · · ● ● ● · · · ·

Two

Fear Is Not the Boss

For God has not given us a spirit of fear,
but of power and of love and of a sound mind.

2 TIMOTHY 1:7 NKJV

If you're like me, you don't just want to know the promises of God, but you want to know how to walk in those promises and realize your destiny. If we are going to live out the promises of God, we need to push past fear and step out in faith. When we have faith, it opens the door for God to work in our lives.

Often, what disrupts our faith is fear, which holds us back and keeps us from experiencing the promises God has for us. Fear and faith are powerful forces in us and have something in common: They both ask us to believe something is going to happen that we cannot see. Fear shouts that business is slow and we're going to go under. Faith declares that God is supplying all of our needs. Fear whispers that we've been through so much, we're never really going to be happy again. Faith confidently says our best days are still in front of us.

Each of us has to determine in our own heart whether to activate faith or fear in our life. You may set out to accomplish a goal, then along the way you run into some obstacles that look impossible and you feel like giving up. It is in times like that you can either activate your faith or let fear stop you. Maybe you want to apply for a better position at work, but when you find out someone you perceive to be more talented is also applying, you change your mind and don't do it. That's activating fear instead of faith. Don't give up, but rise up. Keep moving forward and believe that you're one step closer to living in the reality of your dream. Those obstacles aren't there to stop you; they are there to develop you and strengthen your resolve. Fear brings with it torment and tries to confuse your plans. It is the enemy of your confidence; don't allow fear to stop you. Sure, it's good to live life responsibly and make conscientious decisions, but when you let fear stop you from enjoying life or meeting your potential, then you're not living God's best.

Maybe you're missing out on God's victory and freedom because you keep giving in to fear. If you feel fear today, know that it is not from God. The Scripture says that God is a God of love. He'll give you the strength and resolve you need to move forward despite your fear. Even when, throughout your life, you see opportunities to settle where it is comfortable, resist the urge. God wants to take you higher. You will grow and take possession of your own Promised Land when you take bold steps of faith and embrace the new things God has in store for you.

When Joshua and the entire nation of Israel stood at

the border of the Promised Land, their biggest enemies were not the armies, giants, and barriers into the land; but they were the fear and discouragement that could keep them from God's promise.

"Have I not commanded you? Be strong and courageous. Do not be afraid; do not be discouraged, for the LORD your God will be with you wherever you go."

—JOSHUA 1:9 NIV

God gave Joshua instruction in the simplest of terms: "Do not be afraid. You need to be strong and courageous." God didn't just give Joshua a helpful suggestion, but He gave him a command because He knew the path would be difficult. God said, "Joshua, when you feel fear, don't let it stop you, and don't allow discouragement to defeat you."

Like Joshua, you may have barriers standing in your way. You may perceive that your coworker in the office is the reason you can't get ahead or that your spouse is the reason for your lack of joy. Perhaps you think if you just had better finances you could get ahead. We are all guilty of creating these self-defeating scenarios, but at their very root is fear. What God said to Joshua, He is saying to you today: "Do not be afraid. I will be with you wherever you go." Remember, the power that is in you is greater than the power of fear. When thoughts come that say, *You're not able*, activate your faith by saying, "I can do all things through Christ." Choose faith, overcome fear, and live fearlessly in the freedom God has already given you.

. . . .

Heavenly Father,
I thank You for standing by Your promises. I will overcome fear and discouragement and let my faith arise. I believe I can do all things through Christ Jesus because Your Word says I can. I'm going to live fearlessly in the freedom You have given me and move toward my Promised Land knowing that You are always with me.

In Jesus' name,
Amen

Three

· · · · · ● ● ● · · · ·

Enjoy the Simple Things

*This is the day the L*ORD *has made;*
we will rejoice and be glad in it.

PSALM 118:24 NLT

Joel and I were walking in the park one crisp fall afternoon, taking in the beautiful surroundings. I noticed a leaf floating through the air. It was dancing on the wind in what seemed like slow motion, and with such a carefree spin, as if to say, "Catch me if you can." About that time, I saw Joel leap forward to catch the leaf. He grabbed at the air twice before he finally caught that little leaf. He looked at me with the biggest grin of accomplishment on his face and said, "This is one of my favorite things to do; I used to catch leaves all the time when I was a kid." I laughed as I noticed how much inspiration and joy he got from what most people may overlook—the simple act of catching a leaf in the air.

. . . .

When I look at the night sky and see the work of your fingers—the moon and the stars you set in place—what are mere mortals that you should think about them, human beings that you should care for them? Yet you made them only a little lower than God and crowned them with glory and honor. You gave them charge of everything you made, putting all things under their authority—.

—PSALM 8:3–6 NLT

. . . .

Sometimes we don't see the little things in our day that can bring us joy. We tend to only appreciate the exciting occurrence that has captured our attention—the new car, the job promotion, or the summer vacation. But God has filled our world with His beauty, and if we look for it each day and take a moment to appreciate it, then we won't allow the simple pleasures in life to become ordinary.

When I walked into Joel's office not long after our day in the park, I noticed that leaf sitting on his desk. He had placed it there as a reminder to not overlook the small things in life that refresh and inspire him each day.

Maybe you never caught leaves from the air when you were a kid, but do you ever stop in the busyness of the day just to consider God's creation and your place within it? To hear the birds sing, or to pause what you're doing to listen to your children laughing in the next room, or to take in a still, quiet moment? Throughout the day there are many things that we can take for granted or allow to pass us by without even a second thought. If we are not careful, we will miss the simple but pleasurable moments that come with each day. Each day is His, and there is so much to celebrate and enjoy about it if we look for it.

When we are aware of God's beauty in the world around us, and when we take time to enjoy simple pleasures that brighten our day, we experience a joy and delight that feeds our soul. We add value to our day and enrich our life. Life has a way of keeping us consumed with tasks and the pressure to accomplish, but God never intended us to lose the awe and wonder of the blessings all around us. It is time to slow down and breathe in the ordinary pleasures of life, which can bring extraordinary joy and freedom to each day.

. . . .

Heavenly Father,
You created this day, and You have woven into it things to give me joy and refresh me. Help me to slow down and take in the simple blessings of being alive. I want to be aware of the beauty of this day and all the pleasure it holds. I believe that today is the day that You have made, and it is a good day.

In Jesus' name,
Amen

Four

· · · · · ● ● ● · · · ·

Signal Joy

Rejoice in the Lord always.
Again I will say, rejoice.
PHILIPPIANS 4:4, NKJV

Recently, I was talking to a friend who was feeling discouraged. She was going through a divorce and it was really taking a toll on her. I hated to see my friend struggling, and so I encouraged her to find some *joy* through the hardship. I couldn't change the situation, but if I could help her genuinely smile, I knew it would change the atmosphere of her thoughts.

Science has shown that the mere act of smiling can lift your mood and lower stress. In other words, smiling can trick your brain into feeling happy. When you smile, your body chemistry changes; it signals joy and causes you to feel elated.

I wanted to encourage my friend to find her joy, so I began to joke around and ask her about her teeth. I said, "I haven't seen your teeth in a while." I pulled out two pencils and put one in my mouth, lengthwise between my teeth. When I did that, it made the corner of my mouth turn up and put a smile on my face. I began to act silly and mumbled for her to try it. She was gracious enough to do it, too, and as we stood there looking at one another with pencils in our mouths, we began to laugh.

In Greek the word for *rejoice* means "to brighten." That simple exercise of changing facial expression changed my friend's emotions and brightened not only her face but also her outlook. By smiling, it adjusted her mind-set and opened her to the peace God wanted to give. A lightness came into her eyes and she thanked me for the encouragement. Before we parted, she said to me, "I know God will see me through." As she released the joy within, she opened herself to the power of God's promises.

Consider it pure joy…whenever you face trials of many kinds, because you know that the testing of your faith produces perseverance.

—JAMES 1:2–3 NIV

Many times in life we face complications and difficulties. But Jesus gave us insight on how we should fight back. He said, "In this world you're going to face trials of various kinds but be of good cheer for I have overcome the world." He was saying that it's not what goes on around you that gives you joy, but what He has done for you and within you. When the angels announced the arrival of Jesus, they proclaimed "the good news of great joy." That's when joy entered the world. There are hundreds of scriptures that contain the words *happiness, cheer, delight*. God wants us to use these emotions to push up the joy and signal victory over our difficulties.

There is a light of joy inside you. All you have to do is turn it on. We all need to brighten our spirits with the joy Jesus gave us. When God brought the Israelites out from their oppressive captivity in Babylon He said, "You will go out in joy and be led forth in peace" (Isaiah 55:12). He was showing us that if we're going to come out of a dark place, like my friend, we must use joy to deliver us from anxious thoughts, feelings of defeat, and discouragement. Joy is the key—and it's inside us. It never leaves us. In times of fear and tribulations, we need to remind ourselves that we have the strength to draw that joy out. Start simple by putting a smile on your face. Let your mind and body in on the secret. You can *cheer* up because you know the One who overcame. And because He overcame, you will too. Strengthen your life through joy. Practice it every day no matter what you face; don't let life steal your joy. Turn on your joy, and it will help lead you out of the difficulties of life.

. . . .

Heavenly Father,

I know You are in control of my life and are working everything for my good. Thank You that You are my joy and my peace. As I smile in faith, You will renew the joy of my salvation and bring me out of any struggle I am facing. I will cheer up and overcome through the joy that will strengthen me in tough times. You are my strength and my joy.

In Jesus' name,
Amen

Five

Prioritize Your Day

Teach us to number our days,
that we may gain a heart of wisdom.

PSALM 90:12 NIV

We all have what seems like a million things to do each day. Jobs, family chores, and commitments of all kinds. There are so many activities that fill our time. If we are going to see our dreams come to pass, we need to make room for the most important things in our life. We can't spread ourselves so thin that we can't see the goal God put in our heart or how to make it happen.

There is a difference between activity and productivity. I used to think my multitasking was a gift. I was proud that I could keep so many balls in the air, until I realized I was simply burning energy. I was being more active than productive. Sometimes we can allow the less important demands on our time hold us back from doing what matters most. There are so many things these days that can consume our time. We need to make good decisions about how we spend our time and energy. This is going to take discipline and focus. We must take inventory of our life and identify the things that are wasting our precious time. Doing so is really about prioritizing our day and not allowing the clutter of life to crowd out the important things—the things that move us forward.

To illustrate his point about setting life priorities, a professor stood in front of his students, held up a large glass jar, and carefully put three big rocks in it. The rocks filled the jar to the very top of the glass, and he asked his students, "Is the jar full?" They all said, "Yes"; it looked full. Then he took a plastic bucket of gravel and began to pour gravel into the jar, stopping to shake the jar to work the gravel down into the cracks. Then he asked his students, "Is the jar full?" One student said, "Maybe not." Then the professor took a container of sand and poured the sand in, filling in all the empty spaces between the rocks and gravel.

What was his point? It wasn't that no matter how full your life is, you can always fit more into your schedule. He was demonstrating to his students the principle of productivity. His point was that if you put the big rocks in first, all the smaller things will fill in around them. But if you put the gravel and sand in first, you will never have room for the big rocks.

. . . .

In all your ways acknowledge Him, and He shall direct your paths.

—PROVERBS 3:6 NKJV

. . . .

My question is, what are the big rocks, the most important priorities, in your life? Your family, your career, your volunteer work, or your finances? You have to put the big rocks in your life first if you're going to be successful. And one of the big rocks that would benefit all of us is spending time with God. Our "God Rock" should be the first rock.

If you want God to direct your path, if you want Him to crown your efforts with success, He says, "Put Me first." Nobody wants to move in the wrong direction. Nobody wants to waste their time hanging around the wrong people. We want to do the things that are important. We want to be productive. You may have to get up a little earlier, before the children need you, before the emails start pouring in, before the phone starts ringing. But remember, you draw strength, encouragement, and wisdom when you're in God's presence. That's what keeps your life fresh. That's what keeps you moving forward in freedom to do what matters most. So, make the decision to put the God Rock first in your jar of life. He will help you identify what needs to be emptied from your jar and what other big rocks to keep to get the most out of your day.

. . . .

Heavenly Father,

I will put You in first place in my day. You said that if I acknowledge You then my plans would go well. I want to prioritize spending time with You, and to let you set the tone for my day so that it's productive. Help me to make the most out of the time You have given me. You are my main rock, and I will build my life on You.

In Jesus' name,
Amen

Six

. . . . . . ● ● ● . . . .

Always on His Mind

How precious are your thoughts about me,
O God. They cannot be numbered.
I can't even count them;
they outnumber the grains of sand.

PSALM 139:17–18 NLT

One time, Joel's father, John, was at a high school football game with his friend Jessie. They were in the stands watching Jessie's son play in a championship game. The crowd was intense because the score was close. Jessie's son had the ball and he'd stepped to the right and then to the left when two guys tackled him to the ground. Joel's father didn't say a word as the other team cheered. All of a sudden, John felt an elbow in his side and looked at his friend Jessie. With a big smile on his face, Jessie said, "John, did you see my son's two good moves?" While everyone else saw the tackle and the end of the play, Jessie saw his son's two steps in an attempt to get the ball down the field. He was thinking about his son's two good moves.

Have you ever thought about what God thinks about you when you attempt to take the ball down the field of life? Even when we fumble through life, God sees our good moves.

- -

What is man that you are mindful of him, and the son of man that you care for him?

—PSALM 8:4 ESV

- -

The Scripture says that God is constantly thinking about you and me. What an amazing thought—the Creator of the universe always has something on His mind, and that something is you.

So many people today think God is looking down on them, just waiting for them to mess up. But nothing could be further from the truth. When God thinks about you, He's not thinking about your mistakes, failures, or shortcomings. When you make a mistake God isn't counting that thing against you. He's not thinking about what you did wrong; He doesn't throw you out of the game when you don't make the right moves or get tackled on the field of life. The Lord will not cast you off or forsake you. His thoughts toward you are good. He has a bright future in store for you. He wanted you on his team from the start. He picked you as a star player before you could pick Him. God approves of you. He's pleased with you. You may not always make the right choices and your actions may not be the best. But God is still on your side. He is always there to train and work with you to become the best you can be.

The next time you feel down on yourself, don't look through eyes that see you as a failure. That's not how God thinks of you. Look through God's eyes of love; He is not mad at you, but He is madly in love with you. Receive His love for you in a fresh new way and let it build you into a strong and confident version of yourself, because you are always on his mind.

. . . .

Heavenly Father,

Thank you for Your great love toward me. Even before the foundations of the world, You looked into eternity and saw me personally. Your heart of love and compassion opened toward me and You deliberately chose me that I might know You. Help me to understand Your unconditional love for me so I can walk empowered, grow every day, and move forward into my destiny.

In Jesus' name,
Amen

Seven

· · · · · ● ● ● · · · · ·

Guard Your Heart

Put away the old person you used to be…
Let your minds and hearts be made new.

EPHESIANS 4:22–23 NIV

I was driving to the grocery store one day when I noticed the check engine light on my dashboard came on. This light indicated that my vehicle system was not operating properly. My car appeared to be running normally, so I was tempted to ignore the light, because I was busy and had a lot of errands to do that day. However, I knew ignoring the check engine light could negatively impact the life of my car and result in costly repairs. The light coming on meant there was trouble somewhere in the engine, the heart of the car. I pulled into a gas station and had the mechanic take a look at it for me. It turned out that the problem was minor and all I had to do was add oil to my car. Taking a few minutes to adjust the minor problem saved me from major difficulties later.

If only we had warning lights that would flash in our everyday life when they detect wrong attitudes and thoughts; they could save us from potential problems in our relationships, jobs, and self-esteem. Wouldn't it be great if in much the same way that my engine light was illuminated, a "check heart" light would flash in our minds, so we, too, could pull over and make some adjustments in our attitudes?

King Solomon was known to be the wisest man in

the entire world. He shared his wisdom through the Proverbs in Scripture. One of the many proverbs he wrote concerned his heart. He said:

. . . .

Above all else, guard your heart, for everything you do flows from it.

—PROVERBS 4:23 NIV

. . . .

This wise king told us that the most important part of our life is what goes on in our heart. He knew very well that the heart set the course for our life. In the same way everything flows through the engine of a car to keep it in top condition, everything in our life flows from our heart. Our heart regulates our life. It's the center of who we are, and the condition of our heart determines how we think, speak, and act.

Being able to maintain a positive perspective enhances how we experience life. Guarding our heart from negative thoughts and beliefs is key to enjoying our life. We must be "Heart Care Aware." Dwelling on the bad things that have happened to us or replaying in our mind what someone said or did can cause negativity to take root in our heart. It changes the way we see people and it has a direct impact on how we interact with others in our relationships and careers, and in the way we view our lives. We're going to have stronger relationships and be more content professionally when we can handle criticism instead of getting a chip on our shoulder, or when we can celebrate the victories of others without viewing them as failures of our own.

The experiences we have impact our thoughts and affect our heart. We all struggle at times with negativity, self-doubt, pride, or anger. Someone tried to tear us down and we let that seed take up space in our heart, or we're feeding a belief that we're not likeable. These negative thoughts fuel attitudes that are damaging. But they can be uprooted—God wants us to replace them by knowing that he is working in our lives. And when we guard our heart, we are guarding our life. He is fighting our battles for us. We don't have to fight against everything that comes against us. We need to fight for our heart, not against our heart. We must protect it and take care of what we allow to take root and have precedence in it.

Another important reason we must guard our hearts

Anythink Huron Street
9417 HURON STREET
Thornton 80260
Tel.   303-452-7534
ithink@anythinklibraries.org
https://www.anythinklibraries.org

Date   05/03/2021 16:55:16

Renewed: Fearless & free : inspirational thought
33021035055398
        Due date: 05/24/2021

Renewed: The way of integrity : finding the path
33021035654877
        Due date: 05/24/2021

Renewed: Millennagram : the enneagram guide for
33021032039866
        Due date: 05/24/2021

---

is because uncontrolled negative thoughts can grow and can wreak havoc in our lives. A friend told me about a minor chore her husband neglects around the house that causes daily arguments. Even as she shared with me, she was getting so worked up. I could see that allowing herself to be preoccupied with her husband's flaw had created an attitude within her, and that attitude was now a filter through which she measured her husband's performance as a spouse. When we talked about how she and her husband had gotten to where they are, she realized how toxic her thought pattern had become in this area. She didn't want to have negative thoughts toward her husband. She now realized she was letting what was a small inconvenience in her life become a big problem in her relationship. She began to make some adjustments in her thinking. Every time she felt those negative thoughts creeping in, she chose to turn them around. After about a week of guarding her mind from negative thoughts, she had a change in her heart and it became easier for her to see her husband and their marriage from a positive perspective. That one small adjustment made a big impact in her life.

Our lives move in the direction of our most prominent thoughts. That's why we have to set our minds on what is good, so that we can experience God's blessings and rise higher.

When you feel weak, I want you to pause. Ask yourself if your thoughts are strong and positive. Is negativity seeping into your mind? Are your thoughts productive? Would they be pleasing to God? Are they making your outlook worse than it should be? God wants you to see what He sees. As you begin to guard your heart from negativity and meditate on His goodness, He will renew your thinking. It won't be easy. God never said it would be, but when you're intentional about protecting your heart and practice positive thinking each day, God will lead you to His blessings.

You have the power to change your life by changing your thoughts. If you need victory today, start thinking overcoming thoughts. If you're feeling low, set your mind on things above. If thoughts of defeat are trying to push their way in, push back with the positive thoughts of an overcomer. Don't let the thoughts that attack your heart and life take up residence in you. Let God fight your battles and let them go. As Scripture says, if God is for you who can be against you? He overcame and so can you when you guard your heart.

. . . .

Heavenly Father,
Thank You for showing me how to guard my heart
today and for giving me freedom from the negativity
that tries to take root and darken my attitude. Help
me to see the good in my life and those around me
and to focus on Your blessings. I want my mind to be
filled with things that are good and honorable.

In Jesus' name,
Amen

· · · · · **●** ● · · · ·

Eight

Trust in God's Hands

Surely the arm of the LORD is not too short to save, nor his ear too dull to hear.

ISAIAH 59:1 NIV

I was talking to a woman who was telling me that she and her daughter had been at odds for quite some time. She admitted that when she reflects on their past relationship, she made some bad choices concerning the way she treated her daughter years ago. As the tears rolled down her face, I couldn't help but feel the pain she was experiencing. She wanted so badly to reconcile that relationship but felt like it was out of her control. I asked her if I could pray for her and she nodded and said "yes" in a soft whisper. As I began to pray for her I heard myself say, "God, she feels like her hands are tied and she has done all she can do. But we know, God, that even when our hands are tied, Yours never are."

There is a story in the Bible where three Hebrew teenagers were about to be thrown into the fiery furnace because they wouldn't bow down to the king's golden idol. The guards tied their hands and feet with chords. They were thrown bound into the furnace. There was no hope. The furnace was so hot it even killed the guard who threw them in. They should have instantly been killed, but in a few minutes, when the king came to check on them, he saw them alive in the furnace, and they weren't alone.

Just like the Hebrew boys' hands were tied, you may

feel like your hands are tied. Sometimes we can bring situations on ourselves by the choices we make, or we can find ourselves in a tough situation because of someone else's bad choices. Either way, at times it may seem like you've reached your limit and your circumstances look impossible. You may feel as if things are not going to work out. The good news is that God's hands are not tied. He's not limited by what's limiting you. Whatever seems to be limiting you—a bad relationship, addiction, or financial trouble—God's power to help rescue you is limitless.

. . . .

Then King Nebuchadnezzar was very surprised and stood up in a hurry. He said to his leaders, "Did we not throw three men who were tied up into the fire?" They answered, "That is true, O king." He said, "Look. I see four men loose and walking about in the fire without being hurt. And the fourth one looks like…the Son of God."

—DANIEL 3:24–25 NLV

. . . .

As I prayed for the woman at odds with her daughter, her countenance changed, and she told me she had been filled with hope. She didn't have all the answers yet, but she was able to rise up in faith with a new perspective of God's limitless power in her life. She left that day knowing that God was working in her life, even if she couldn't see how things could be turned around.

Maybe you find yourself in a difficult situation today. You don't know how it will work out. Remember, God's hands are never tied. The fourth man has shown up. Like the Hebrew teenagers, you're coming out of that fire. Not only are God's hands free to help you today, they are stretched out toward you, inviting you to come and find rest in Him. God can turn any situation around in your life. He can open doors; He can soften hard hearts and give you the favor you need. Even when you can't see a way, God has a way. Your job is not to try to figure it all out but to trust Him and move forward in faith. See yourself free; believe you're rising to new levels and breaking bad habits. Ask God to help restore your relationships so that you have a happy family and a great marriage. Do what you can do, but trust God when it's out of your control. God can do the impossible. His hands are always free to work good things in your life, and He can do the impossible.

. . . .

Heavenly Father,

I come to You today, giving You all that I am. I release what I myself cannot change into Your mighty hands. I trust that You are working behind the scenes in my life even when I can't see a way forward. Thank You for Your faithfulness and for strengthening me as I keep my heart and mind focused on You. Your hands are never tied and You are the God of the impossible.

In Jesus' name,

Amen

Nine

· · · · · ● · ● · ● · · · · ·

Attitude of Gratitude

Oh give thanks to the Lord, for he is good;
for his steadfast love endures forever.

PSALM 118:29 ESV

One day as I was meditating on First Thessalonians 5:18, which says, "Give thanks in all circumstances; for this is God's will for you in Christ Jesus" (NIV), I couldn't help but think of all the people facing challenges who might be reading this verse and thinking, *How can I be thankful for this sickness? How can I be thankful for losing my job? How can I be thankful for this unexpected bill?* But as I studied the verse more closely, I realized the Lord isn't saying to be thankful *for* everything; He is saying to be thankful *in* everything. There's a big difference.

When things aren't going the way we expect and we have difficulties, or when we are facing challenging times, it's easy to look at the problem and worry and complain. However, when we use our faith, we choose to be thankful despite the problems. It's easy to look at the trouble, but we need to look at the faithfulness of God. During hard times God is asking us to be thankful for His faithfulness and trust Him to help us face every situation.

It wouldn't make sense to thank God *for* the trouble in your life, but it makes perfect sense to praise Him because He is the *way out* of that trouble. Through Him you can live fearlessly and freely no matter what you're facing. The Scripture gives great promises of God's faithfulness. If you are facing something in your life, find an encouraging

Scripture to meditate on and give thanks for God's faithfulness. If you have lost your job, you can boldly pray: "Thank You, Lord, that You're bringing something better my way, and that You are opening doors no man can shut." Maybe you received an unexpected bill; your attitude should be: "Thank You, God, for being my Provider. Because I am in covenant with You, I know You will supply all of my needs according to Your riches in glory." As you pray the promises of God you will feel faith rise up inside of you, and you'll gain strength that will bring peace to your heart.

. . . .

Do not be anxious about anything, but in every situation, by prayer and petition, with thanksgiving, present your requests to God. And the peace of God, which transcends all understanding, will guard your hearts and your minds in Christ Jesus.

—PHILIPPIANS 4:6–7 NIV

. . . .

When you are thankful, it opens the door for God to move on your behalf. It brings you closer to Him. And when you're close, you'll be able to receive His strength and His courage to walk through any circumstance. That's why we should always have the attitude of gratitude that says, "God, in spite of what's happened, I choose to be grateful."

Gratitude is a choice. You can choose to find something to be grateful for, or you can choose to complain and be miserable. Finding something to be grateful for will change your perception of your situation. You'll think more creatively about how to solve your problems and negative emotions won't drain your energy. Gratefulness opens your heart to the possibilities and gives you the stamina to do what it takes to succeed.

Studies have shown people who deliberately practice gratefulness are happier people.

That means you can get better at being grateful by practicing. The more you practice having a grateful heart, the easier it will be to maintain that attitude of gratitude. Pretty soon, being grateful will become a habit. So, I want to encourage you to be deliberate. If you're not the kind of person who is automatically grateful, determine to become that person. Gratitude can be learned. Looking through the positive lens of gratitude, you will get a vision of something better, which always helps to overcome the temptation to get down and discouraged.

I read an article about a family that went through a devastating storm on the West coast of Florida. They had to evacuate their home because of 14- to 16-foot waves and hurricane-force winds that lasted twelve hours. When they were able to return safely they found that their home had been destroyed and all their possessions had been swept out to sea. The family of six was now living in the home of a loved one. The article told of how, after digging through the debris of the home they had once lived in and loved, they realized more than ever that what they loved most was one another. Instead of letting the loss of their material possessions consume their thoughts and words, they shifted their attention to concentrate on thanking God for all He had done for them and for sparing their lives. Making an effort to be thankful in everything led them to see God's faithfulness in preserving their lives, and they gained a new understanding of what is really important to them.

I encourage you to be grateful on purpose. Make an effort to see the possibilities in a seemingly impossible situation. Maybe start by writing down three things to be grateful for every day. You might be surprised by how much your perspective will change when you start counting your blessings in writing, so you can keep them in front of you. Make a habit of naming what you're thankful for each night before bed. Tape a note to your bathroom mirror to remind yourself what you can appreciate in each day. Speak those things out loud to yourself in the mirror first thing when you get up. You have the power to train your brain to see the good in your life. You may face some ups and downs in life and you may not be happy about everything you are going through right now; however, you will move through difficulties with greater faith if you will look at what you have and not at what you don't have. That will help you be thankful in everything.

· · · · · · · · · · ·

Heavenly Father,

When I am tempted to complain about my situation, help me to keep my eyes on You and be thankful for Your faithfulness in my life. I believe, as I pray with thanksgiving in my heart, that You will make a way for me. I am determined to surrender my way to You and open my heart for You to help me and strengthen me, no matter the circumstances. I know, Lord, that You will take care of me, and You will bless all that concerns me.

In Jesus' name,
Amen

Ten

· · · · · ● ● ● · · · · ·

Faithful with the Small Stuff

*"Whoever can be trusted with very little
can also be trusted with much, and whoever
is dishonest with very little will also
be dishonest with much."*

LUKE 16:10 NIV

When we read about the heroes of faith in the Scriptures, it's like we're seeing a highlights reel of their lives. We are amazed when Moses parts the Red Sea and boldly tells Pharaoh, "Let the Israelites go," but we aren't given the details of his life during the forty years he lived out in the desert of Midian. And when we read about David killing the great giant Goliath with just his slingshot and a smooth stone, we're very impressed. But there isn't much about his many days spent tending his father's sheep. Even in the lives of Moses and David, the miracle days were way fewer than the ordinary days.

Why would we think our lives would be any different?

The truth is, you're going to have many more ordinary days than exciting miraculous days, and that's okay because those ordinary days have purpose. Those ordinary days are preparing you for something greater. When you're being faithful in your routine, doing your best in the ordinary tasks of each day, and when it seems no one is noticing and nothing is changing, just know that God is watching and *you* are changing. See, when you're faithful in the ordinary—showing up on time, putting in the hours, and working with a good attitude— God is developing your character and preparing you for promotion.

You'll never become all you were created to be without being your best during the mundane seasons of life. When God can trust you to be faithful in the ordinary, then He can trust you with the extraordinary. That's why it's important to learn to enjoy where God has you right now, knowing that He is doing a work *in* you so He can work *through* you.

That's exactly what happened to a friend of mine who thought her job of writing letters for her company was dull and unimportant. Yet she kept doing her job to the best of her abilities for years. Then, one day she received a call from a recipient of one of her letters. He specifically asked for her when he phoned the company because she had signed the letters on behalf of the organization. He told her he had appreciated her correspondence, and she went on to assist him with what he needed.

To my friend, it seemed like just another ordinary day of being faithful, but she had just walked into the extraordinary. That man ended up introducing her to a doctor who was able to give her sister a lifesaving liver transplant—all because she was faithful in her work even though it felt boring and insignificant. Being faithful in the ordinary set her up for a divine appointment that saved her sister's life and changed their family forever.

Like my friend, you may feel there is more on the inside of you, yet nobody seems to notice your hard work or your abilities. In the eyes of the world, it may look as though you're no closer to your dreams than you were several years ago, but when you do the ordinary with a good attitude, you're patient when it takes longer than anticipated, and you have faith when you're not getting your way, you will be both transformed and rewarded. You're showing God that you trust Him in the mundane and the magnificent, in the valley and on the mountaintop. You are showing Him that you are ready for more, so stay faithful during that preparation season.

That's what David had to do. He was anointed to be king thirteen years before he actually took the throne. Meanwhile, he was faithful in the ordinary, simply tending his father's sheep. He knew he was called to rule a nation, yet he was stuck in a field full of livestock. He wasn't "living the dream," but he knew the dream was coming, so he kept being the best shepherd he could be until that season in his journey was over. He had the attitude, "I'm not working for people, not my brothers or even my earthly father. I'm working for my Heavenly Father, so I'm giving it my all."

When you, like David, adopt this commitment to faithfulness, you will take your throne. Are you being excellent where God has you now? You see, it's not the big things that hold most people back. It's the little things, the ordinary things. If you can't be faithful in the little things, God knows you aren't ready for the big things that He has in store for you. So, let's be faithful every day, no matter what season we're in. Let's be our best and live fearlessly and freely with a song of praise in our hearts.

. . . .

"'Well done, good and faithful servant. You have been faithful with few things; I will put you in charge of many things. Come and share your master's happiness.'"

—MATTHEW 25:23 NIV

. . . .

If you'll learn to enjoy where God has you right now, God will make things happen that you couldn't make happen on your own, and you'll cross over from the ordinary to the extraordinary.

. . . .

Heavenly Father,

Thank you for all the days of my life, both the ordinary and the extraordinary. Help me to have a good attitude when things aren't moving as quickly as I'd like and help me to be excellent in all I do, even when it seems like my work goes unnoticed. I know that You are watching over me and preparing me for exceptional days ahead. Lord, help me to keep growing, serving, and being my best where I am now so that I can be ready for where You are taking me. I love You and I trust You.

In Jesus' name,
Amen

Eleven

Go to God with Your Mistakes

If we confess our sins, he is faithful and just and will forgive us our sins and purify us from all unrighteousness.

1 JOHN 1:9 NIV

One Saturday afternoon when I was sixteen years old, my dad was grilling hamburgers and needed some things from the store. I had just gotten my license and, knowing I would gladly run the errand for him, he gave me his list and said, "Go straight to the store, get the groceries, and then come straight home." Then he said, "By the way, the passenger-side window is broken and off track. Don't open it until I get it fixed."

"Okay, Dad," I said with a kiss and a smile as I headed out the door. And as any good sixteen-year-old-girl would do, I went straight to my best friend's house down the street and picked her up. Being the responsible young lady that I was, I told her to be careful about the window. Well, we drove about one block when we saw a boy we knew walking down the street and wanted to say Hi. After all, he was walking and we were driving. We pulled up and I said to my friend, "Roll down the window and say hello." She responded, "But I thought your dad said not to use the window." Caught up in the moment, I said, "Oh, it will be okay one time. Just do it slowly."

My friend rolled down the window, and we started waving and acting so cool. Everything was great until my friend tried to raise the window. Suddenly, it was like the world stopped as I watched the window shatter into a million pieces. "Oh, no!" I cried. I would have given anything to turn back the clock at that moment.

I looked at that window and looked at my friend. I said, "You are coming home with me." I knew I needed her to be my backup as I faced my dad. We drove straight to my house in complete silence. The walk up our driveway wasn't nearly long enough as I tried to figure out how to explain to my dad what had just happened. I slowly walked inside with my friend—the one who wasn't supposed to be with me. My dad was in the kitchen when he turned and saw us. You can imagine the puzzled look on his face. "Dad, I'm so sorry…" I started to say, barely knowing how to explain.

. . . .

He does not treat us as our sins deserve or repay us according to our iniquities…As a father has compassion on his children, so the LORD has compassion on those who fear him.

—PSALM 103:10,13 NIV

. . . .

Because I knew my father loved me, I had the confidence to tell him the whole story. When I admitted to my dad that I had disobeyed him, he forgave me. Of course he was disappointed, but it didn't change his love for me. He didn't hold it over my head or measure my worth or value by that mistake. He didn't disconnect his heart from me and I didn't retreat from his love.

My dad's love that day was an example of our Heavenly Father's love. Maybe you weren't raised with a dad like mine and it's hard to believe that God is that forgiving. It doesn't matter how many times you have blown it; God is always ready to receive you with open arms. When we come to Him with our mistakes, He embraces us and forgives us. Don't run from God; turn to God. He is always there to give us another chance. God is full of love and mercy. Don't let fear hold you back when you make a mistake. There is freedom when you confess your faults to Him; He always wants to hear from you. Go to Him and allow His love to renew and restore you today.

. . . .

Heavenly Father,
I know Your Love goes way beyond any human love I have ever experienced. I believe You are patient and kind and always forgiving. Forgive me for any wrongs

today. I come to You, not hiding anything from You and I thank You that You are a good Father. You love me just the way I am and because of that I want to obey You in all I do. I want to embrace this fundamental truth that You are not mad at me but madly in love with me. Keep me close to You and strengthen me day by day, so I can please You and become all You want me to be.

In Jesus' name,
Amen

· · · · · ● ● ● · · · ·

Twelve

Embrace
the Season

He has made everything beautiful in its time.
He has also set eternity in the human heart;
yet no one can fathom what God
has done from beginning to end.

ECCLESIASTES 3:11 NIV

My favorite season has always been spring. It's so beautiful with all of the flowers and trees in bloom. But you know what? You can't have spring without first going through winter.

As I write this book, it's wintertime where I live, and when I look outside, the grass is brown, the flowers appear dead, and the trees are leafless. Everything looks lifeless. Horticulturists tell us there is a lot going on during this dormant season. The nutrients that the trees, flowers, and plants need to grow and bloom are resourced into different areas of the vegetation in preparation for spring growth and blooming. Unless this takes place, the trees and plants will not become what they're supposed to be.

And neither will we. You see, during the times when we feel as though there's nothing happening, as though we're dormant, we need to be pushing patience, faithfulness, and steadfastness to the other areas of our lives. Then, when it's time to go to the next level, when it's time for new growth, we will be ready to bud and eventually bloom.

Ecclesiastes 3 begins with this verse: "To everything there is a season, a time for every purpose under heaven." We serve an eternal God but everything under the sun on this earth has a season and a time.

Some seasons are easier to mark in time than others. For example, when a baby is born, that baby goes from an infant to a toddler rather quickly. Then, one day that toddler gets up and goes to the first grade. That same child grows up and goes to college, then enters the workforce, and then has his and her own family. You can mark those seasons in time and you can see the growth. And, if everything has gone as it should, every season will have prepared him or her for the next season.

In life, each season has a purpose, and each season is important, but too often we fail to understand the purpose and importance of the season we're in—especially if it's a particularly difficult one. We spend our days wishing away the very season God is using to grow us and shape us for His plan.

Not every season is a fun one, but you don't quit living or moving forward simply because it's tough. Instead, you've got to embrace the season and squeeze everything out of it so you'll be prepared to go to the next season. You've got to make the decision to thrive in it, not just survive it.

That's what Joseph did. The Scriptures tell us that he was the favorite child in his family, and that his eleven brothers were very jealous of him—so jealous, in fact, they plotted to kill him. One day, the brothers ambushed him and threw him in a pit. Then one of the brothers pleaded on Joseph's behalf, and instead of killing him they sold him into slavery.

That was a difficult season, but soon after, Joseph was taken to Egypt and sold to a high-ranking official named Potiphar. Because Joseph embraced his season and worked hard for Potiphar, he excelled. But that season of favor was short-lived.

Potiphar's wife noticed Joseph and tried to seduce him, and when he rejected her advances, she lied to her husband about what had actually happened. Joseph ended up in prison. But that isn't the end of his story. Joseph found favor in prison, embracing his present season, and rose again in great victory. One bad season after another, he just kept on growing. From the pit to the prison to the palace, Joseph stayed faithful to God, and God blessed him beyond his wildest dreams. He didn't die on the vine during those growing seasons, and you won't either. You're going to use those difficult seasons to grow and become everything God has called you to be.

I want you to be encouraged today and start enjoying

life right where you are. I want you to wake up every morning thinking, *These are the good old days*, appreciating whatever season you're in. There's an old quote that says, "Yesterday is history, tomorrow is a mystery, but today is a gift." That's why it's called "the present." I like that, don't you? Today really is a gift, but we have to see it that way. Maybe you're not where you'd like to be in life but look how far you've already come. God is doing big things in you and through you, and He has more in store.

. . . .

For his anger lasts only a moment, but his favor lasts a lifetime; weeping may stay for the night but rejoicing comes in the morning.

—PSALM 30:5 NIV

. . . .

It's easy to make the mistake of longing for what used to be or rushing ahead for what will be, but if you'll learn everything you can where you are now, you won't just *go* through it; you'll *grow* through it. Remember, you're in a time of preparation. Own the season you're in, but don't get stuck there. No matter how long or difficult it seems,

I promise you, this too will pass. Just like winter gives way to spring, better days are in your future.

seasons

waiting

. . . .

Heavenly Father,

Help me to embrace every season—even the difficult ones—knowing that You are preparing me for something greater. I want to learn everything You want me to learn and to not just go through this season but to grow through it. Father, don't let me miss a blooming season because I'm stuck in the past or longing for easier, better days. I want to move forward with You and become all that You have created me to be. Help me to trust You more, Lord. I love You.

In Jesus' name,

Amen

Thirteen

Let Your Light Shine

*"You are the light of the world…Let your light
shine before others, so that they may
see your good works and give glory
to your Father who is in heaven."*

MATTHEW 5:14–16 ESV

There was a little boy whose father bought him a new flashlight. He took it outside on a bright sunny day, turned it on, and shined it around, but he couldn't see any light coming from the flashlight. He said, "Daddy, it doesn't work, something's wrong with this flashlight." "No, Son, it's fine," his father said. "It wasn't designed to work in the light; it was made to work in the darkness. That's when you'll see what it can really do. It's in the dark that you see the light shine."

Sometimes we find ourselves in dark and unpleasant situations and it's easy to complain. *I don't like this job. These people are so negative. Nobody has a good attitude.* But it is in times like these when we need the light. These are opportunities for us to shine. I've heard it said we can either be a thermometer and measure the temperature, or we can be a thermostat and change the temperature. When you hear people complaining about the company, don't join in: "Yeah, it's really bad around here." Be a thermostat and turn it around by saying, "Things may not be perfect, but I'm grateful that I have a job. I'm thankful that I can come to work each day." You were designed to shine and to illuminate what's good. You are the light of the world, so don't add to the darkness; turn your light on. It works best in the dark places. When you're around negative influences, gossiping, complaining, or people playing politics, don't turn your light off, don't hide; let it shine brightly.

- -

We are ambassadors for Christ.

—2 CORINTHIANS 5:20 NKJV

- -

We have to realize people can't see God, but they see us. The question is, are we making God look good? Are we representing Him the right way, as His ambassadors? Do people want what we have? To live fearless and free is to let your light shine with your actions, not just with your words.

Parents, we can tell our children, "Be kind. Be respectful." But if they see us being disrespectful or not treating people right, our words will go in one ear and out the other. The power to represent Christ to others is in what we do. Some people are not reading their Bibles, but they are reading our life. Some may never come to church or listen to a minister, but they're watching how we live. We should have so much joy and peace, and we should be so kind, generous, and good-natured that people want what we have. That's what it means to be the light of the world.

Remember, your actions speak louder than your words. Your life is your message, and when you're in those dark places, don't complain. Try to have a new perspective and realize that in those tough situations are opportunities for your light to shine brightly so you can be a positive influence to others. If you'll put this simple principle into action, shining your light brightly in the darkness, you'll not only make a difference in other people's lives, but you'll experience a remarkable difference in your own life and outlook.

. . . .

Heavenly Father,

I believe You have given me the power to shine brightly everywhere I am. When it seems dark and things get tough, give me the strength to be the light and shine in every situation. I want to be a beacon of hope to a hurting world. I know I can do this, as You help me to be fearless in representing You and free to show Your goodness to everyone I meet.

In Jesus' name,
Amen

· · · · · **●** ● ● · · · · ·

Fourteen

God Is Certain of Your Abilities

*We are more than conquerors and gain
a surpassing victory through Him Who loved us.*

ROMANS 8:37 AMPC

I read a story about a boxer who hired a world-renowned trainer to make him into a champion. The trainer believed in the ability of this young boxer and was eager to help him become the champion he knew he could be. The boxer worked hard at drills and trained at a high level to prepare. But his uncertainty about whether he could win fights was affecting his performance in the ring. In order to boost his confidence, the trainer began to write a number on a small slip of paper and place it inside the boxer's glove. That may sound like a strange thing to give a boxer right before a fight, but he had a reason for what he did. The number that he wrote on that slip of paper was the round in which he predicted his boxer would knock out his opponent. It showed that he had so much confidence in the boxer's ability, the question became not *whether* he would win, but in which round. This had such a positive effect on the young boxer's thinking that he found a new confidence in his ability to win fights. Because of his trainer's ability to bring out the best in him he became known as Muhammad Ali, heavyweight champion of the world. Confidence played a tremendous part in Ali's success as one of the greatest boxers that ever lived. His trainer, Angelo Dundee, was certain of his boxer's ability to succeed, and that confidence in Ali gave him a champion's mentality. That piece of paper in Ali's glove was just a number. It did nothing until it became a part of his thinking. In much the same way Dundee believed in Ali, the God who holds the universe in the palm of His hand has faith in you.

Remember the young woman in the Scripture named Esther, who became an orphan as a young girl and her life held little hope for significance. The odds that she'd ever have an opportunity to make much of a difference with her life were against her. However, Esther had a cousin, Mordecai, who deposited words of faith and hope in her heart. He could see in her the ability to rise up out of a difficult life and do something great. It was that voice of victory and those words of encouragement that helped Esther recognize her value and develop the confidence she needed to fulfill her destiny. Because of the seeds of confidence Mordecai had deposited into her life, when King Xerxes was looking for a new queen, Esther was able to put her fear behind her, step up, and experience God's favor in the palace of the king. She not only saw God's hand of blessing on her life, but because she didn't shrink back, she gained the courage to boldly face down the enemy of her people and realize her potential as a queen. When you start to think of yourself in terms of how God sees you, there will be no question about whether you'll win.

You may not be a professional boxer, or in the running to become a queen or king of a nation, but if you look inside yourself you will find that God has planted seeds of greatness in you. He has called you a champion. You are royalty in His eyes. You, too, can develop a fearless confidence because the Creator of the Universe has put in you everything you need to win in life. He is on your side and in your corner. Wherever you go you have the favor of God. It is not a matter of *whether* you will overcome but *when* you will gain the victory. Even when you're not always certain of the outcomes in your life, God is. You don't have to be held back by fear because He knows your ability to succeed.

. . . .

What shall we say about such wonderful things as these?
If God is for us, who can ever be against us?

—ROMANS 8:31 NLT

. . . .

Embrace this truth today and let it take root in your heart. No person, no lack, no fear, can stand against the freedom and victory God has in store for your life. Keep yourself in an atmosphere of faith by allowing God to be your trainer. Let His words deposit confidence in you. Go through the preparation to become all that you are intended to be. God will help you to develop the champion in you.

. . . .

Heavenly Father,

I believe that You are in my corner cheering me on. I will continue to grow and develop into the champion You have made me to be. I will not allow uncertainty to hold me back. I will have confidence that You have destined me to win, and my greatest victories are still in my future. I walk in the favor and blessing You have put on my life and will not stop until I see victory.

In Jesus' name,
Amen

Fifteen

· · · · · **·** **·** · · · ·

Delight in
the Lord

*Delight yourself in the L*ORD *and he will
give you the desire of your heart.*

PSALM 37:4 ESV

What you delight in shapes your desires. God wants to give you the desires of your heart as you build a relationship with Him. He not only wants to put desires in your heart, but he wants to nurture the ones you already have.

It's in the difficult times when we ask the question, "Do the desires of my heart align with God's desires for my life?" There was a young lady whose boyfriend broke up with her after having dated seriously for one and a half years. He felt like he needed time to grow as a man in many areas of his life and didn't want to be in a serious relationship any longer. She told how she felt confused and was so heartbroken. They had decided to leave the relationship open-ended and let time tell if or when they would get back together. After struggling with her feelings, she came to the conclusion that it was best to surrender her desire to the Lord and ask Him to help her as she moved forward in her life. Although she knew what she desired, she entrusted it to God and asked Him to work in her life. She revealed how, day after day, for eight months she meditated on Psalm 37:4.

She kept her Bible with her everywhere she went. She read it in her spare time, sometimes soaking up comfort and other times simply marveling over the goodness of God. She found herself enjoying her time talking to God, and her prayer life grew by leaps and bounds. She began to see small prayers answered and grew in her faith to pray bigger ones. God began to place new desires in her heart. She made new friends and began to bring them to church with her. She explained how her desire to get back with her boyfriend wasn't the primary focus of her life, and she became more content and joyful while falling in love with God in a new way.

About a year later, she and her boyfriend did get back together and decided to rebuild their relationship. Not only did he grow during their time apart, but because she surrendered her desire to God, she grew as well. Today they are married and have two beautiful children. God not only gave her the desire of her heart, but in the process, He became the desire of her heart. Now she can live fearlessly and freely in loving her family and giving them her very best. From her experience of surrendering her relationship to God, she now has the desire to give her time and attention to what God wants to do in her and through her.

She recognizes the importance of putting God first in her life. When you delight yourself in God, He will shape in you His desire and give you the passion and faith to see those dreams come to pass in your life.

. . . .

The heart regulates the hands.

—2 CORINTHIANS 8:12 MSG

. . . .

In his letter to the Corinthians, it was Paul who said the heart regulates the hands, meaning that what you have in your heart is what you are going to put your hands to. Your hands and your heart work together just like delight and desire. My friend discovered that her heart regulates her hands. Instead of struggling with her emotions, she gave her desires to God. She then put her hands to the work that He had for her.

What you've allowed to form in your heart is what you pursue, what you work toward, and what you have passion for. Power flows into your relationships, your desires, and your dreams when your heart is committed.

Do you want to see your desires materialize? Then consider the things you're investing in and what it is you're delighting in. Ask God to mold your passions and to align the work of your hands and heart with His. Take the time to invest and delight in the Lord, and He will shape your desires to align with His.

God wants your heart to be His garden and to cultivate within you passion and purpose. Delight in His presence by reading His Word. Get to know what He says about you. Spend time with Him and sing songs of praise-making music in your heart.

Throughout the day, you can talk to God about your decisions, bringing Him into your everyday life. He is concerned about what concerns you and wants to guide you and give you wisdom and counsel. God is a good God. He is not mad at you; He is madly in love with you. He wants to surprise you with what He can do through you. When you take delight in Him, He will unlock more than the fulfillment of your dreams; He will unlock the power of His miracles in your life.

. . . .

Heavenly Father,
I want to pursue the best plans You have for my life and fearlessly invest my heart in the things that please You. Help me to put You in the first-place position

in my life, so You can shape my desire as I delight in You. Thank You for planting Your purposes in my heart and accomplishing great things in and through me. Let me have a heart for the things of Heaven. I want to be close to You and love the things You love. I believe that the desires You plant in my heart will be fulfilled and I patiently anticipate Your miracles in my life.

In Jesus' name,
Amen

Sixteen

No Filter Needed

"For I know the plans I have for you,"
declares the LORD, "plans to prosper you…
to give you hope and a future."

JEREMIAH 29:11 NIV

The other day, I was scrolling through my social media feed and looking at the amazing and fun photos posted by friends and family. Then I started thinking about all the ways we "enhance" our photos. We have filters and apps that add makeup, or that make us look thinner, taller, or younger, and there are even apps that make us look like silly creatures. It's funny how, in our culture, we've become so absorbed in the way we present ourselves. We make sure we only post the very best of the best images.

The good news is that God doesn't need you to put a filter on your life. You don't have to worry that He won't like what He sees; He doesn't need you to download an app that makes you look better. He doesn't accept you only when you are perfect or judge you when you fail. His acceptance isn't based on your performance. He loves you just the way you are and has plans for you.

We all have days when life tries to knock us out and get us off track. The world definitely makes it easy not to appreciate who you are. High work demands to be successful, unrealistic media standards of attractiveness, and a culture of sharing and comparing is enough to wear on your self-esteem. The world tells you that you need to be perfect—the perfect mom, dad, student, employee, or even the perfect Christian. You should be the best and the first at everything. Juggle it all, do it with grace, and look good while you're doing it. Maybe you've even suffered the belittlement of others or have experienced things that have made you question whether you are worthy of being loved. But that's not God's thoughts toward you. His thoughts are for your good.

For you created my inmost being; you knit me together in my mother's womb. I praise you because I am fearfully and wonderfully made; your works are wonderful, I know that full well.

—PSALM 139:13–14 NIV

If your child or someone you care about came to you weary, full of doubt about their worth, and struggling to love themselves amidst today's pressures, what would you tell them? Would you remind them how precious they are? Help them see that they're wonderful just the way they are? What your heart would want for them is what the Father wants you to know about yourself—you are wonderful just the way you are. He says you are fearfully and wonderfully made. When God designed you, He put in you everything you need to fulfill your destiny. Everything is right about you. Whether you're a high-powered CEO or a mom shuffling through the first months of your baby's life, sleep-deprived and in sweatpants, you matter to God and are His beautiful creation. Hold fast to that truth about what God declares over you.

God wants you to know who you are and whose you are. He wants you to set an example for others to follow. The way you live your life matters. How you see yourself is important because others follow your lead. Your greatest asset is a healthy self-esteem. When you value what God has placed in your life, knowing that you are growing and becoming the person He wants you to be, you reflect that same value on others. Don't pretend everything is perfect or try to put filters on your life, become fearless and free to be the authentic *you*. Your unique personality and characteristics are qualities people need. You can inspire others just by believing in yourself and living at your personal best. Start today believing that God has you and your situation in the palm of his hand. He is on your side and is cheering you on. I encourage you to begin to see yourself the way God sees you. He doesn't need a filter to approve you so start approving yourself. You may not be where you want to be in life. But you are where you are supposed to be.

Embrace your life today; live in the freedom that comes from knowing that God loves you unconditionally. Get up every morning and start with a declaration of faith: "I am God's masterpiece, and He loves me today just the way I am." Let the love of God build confidence in you, and boldly go out and be all that He has created you to be.

. . . .

Heavenly Father,

I want to see myself the way You see me. I don't want to get my value from the culture I live in or the opinions of others. I want to know Your love in my heart so I can reflect it to others. Thank You that it isn't my perfection, or the way I perform, that qualifies me in Your eyes. It is the fact that I am Your child and You dearly love me. I accept Your love today, and I will build my strength and confidence in that love. Thank You that I am becoming better every day, in every way. I love You.

In Jesus' name,
Amen

· · · · · **·** **·** **·** · · · ·

Seventeen

God Is Breathing on You

The angel answered, "The Holy Spirit will come on you, and the power of the Most High will overshadow you…"

LUKE 1:35 NIV

You may have heard the story of Jesus' birth many times, but have you ever really stopped to imagine what it must have been like for Mary? She was just a humble teenage girl living in Nazareth. Nazareth was one of the poorest, most rundown cities of that region; nothing of any notoriety had taken place there. One day, an angel appeared with news that would change Mary's life.

"Do not be afraid, Mary; you have found favor with God. You will conceive and give birth to a son, and you are to call him Jesus."

—LUKE 1:30–31 NIV

God gave Mary this amazing promise that wasn't even believable in the natural. You can imagine the thoughts of doubt and disbelief that must have bombarded her mind. Thoughts like, *How can I have a baby without a man? That's impossible. That defies the laws of nature.* If Mary had considered her circumstances, she certainly would have been tempted to not believe what God spoke to her. But instead of looking at her circumstances, she looked to God. She understood this principle: If God says it, He will bring it to pass.

Mary's reply to the angel wasn't "How could this happen?" She didn't say, "Oh, that sounds too far out. I don't see how that can happen." She didn't question God's message. No, Mary was bold. She made a statement of faith. She said, "Be it unto me even as you have said." In other words, "I'm going to get into an agreement with God. Let it happen. If God says I'm highly favored, I believe it. If God says the impossible is going to happen, I believe it." That's the way we need to be when God puts a promise in our heart. Instead of trying to reason it out, we have to be fully convinced that what He said, He will do.

Mary believed but she did have one question. She answered the angel and said, "I believe this promise will come to pass. I'm in agreement. But how is this going to happen?"

You may have a "how" in your life right now. In other words, you may be thinking, *I believe I'm going to accomplish my dreams, but how am I going to do it? How am I going to get well? How am I going to overcome this addiction?* What the angel said to Mary in response is true for all of us today. Here's how it's going to happen: through God's power. In other words, God is going to breathe in your direction, and things you couldn't make happen on your own are going to happen. The word "spirit" in that verse is similar to the word "breathe." The breakthroughs that are coming, the healing, the restoration, and the promotion, are because God is shifting the winds and breathing in your direction.

How are you going to accomplish your dreams? The Most High God, the Great I Am, the Creator of the Universe is going to empower you. Problems that looked permanent will turn out to be only temporary. When God breathes in your direction miracles happen.

Instead of considering your circumstances today, why don't you consider your God? The dream He has placed in your heart may seem impossible; it may look too big, but don't overanalyze it or reason it all out. Follow Mary's example. Dare to say, "God, I don't see a way, but I know You have a way. Let it happen to me according to Your Word." Then, take courage and trust that God is working behind the scenes. When thoughts come saying, *It's too late. It's impossible*, learn to ignore them and don't let them keep you from walking in your promise. Don't give them life with your words. That may be one report, but remember God is breathing in your direction. And He has the final say.

Today, just like Mary, don't give up; do your part. Get into agreement with God's Word and receive His promises. Stay faithful and keep honoring and obeying Him, and it won't be long before you see God do what only He can do. He is breathing in your direction today and you will bring forth the promises of God.

. . . .

Heavenly Father,

Thank you, Father, for breathing in my direction. I want to bring forth the promises that You have for my life. I will consider your Power and Ability working in me. Help me to not look at situations and think impossible, *but to look to You, the God of the possible. Just like with Mary, I know that You are in control of everything, and if I remain faithful You will do great things in and through me. I believe the winds of change are blowing in my direction and I am healed, whole, and set free.*

In Jesus' name,
Amen

Eighteen

. . . . . ● . . . . .

Lift Each Other Up

*Do not let any unwholesome talk come
out of your mouths, but only what is helpful for
building others up according to their needs,
that it may benefit those who listen.*

EPHESIANS 4:29 NIV

I heard about a man whose wife was making him breakfast. He asked for two eggs, one scrambled and one fried. She made them and put them on a plate. When he saw them he shook his head. She said, "What did I do wrong now? That's exactly what you asked for." He replied, "I should have known it. You fried the wrong egg."

Too many people go through life focused on what's wrong rather than what's right. We have to be careful not to have a habit of seeing and being drawn to what's negative. It's so important to choose to see the beautiful rose before the thorn. It's easy to notice what's wrong in life, but it takes faith to recognize what's good. Instead of having a critical eye, it's important we develop an eye for spotting what's good.

This is especially crucial in our relationships. Training ourselves to see people's strengths above their weaknesses is what builds good relationships. When we focus on what we like about our spouse and magnify their positive qualities rather than the things that annoy us, we see the good in them and value them for who they are. That's when we can use our words to compliment and encourage them in their life.

Take advantage of opportunities to use your words to

promote the best in others. Remember, it will not only benefit them but it will benefit you. The higher you help others go, the higher God will take you.

Studies say that our minds have a natural tendency to gravitate toward the negative, and that makes it much easier to be a faultfinder. Some people never see the good their spouse does. They've forgotten the reasons they fell in love and got married in the first place. They've fallen out with a parent or friend. It's because they're magnifying the wrong things. If you struggle in this area, I encourage you to make a list of the qualities that you like about your spouse or that person in your life. Write down the things that they do right. He may not be a good communicator but he's a hard worker. Put that on your list. She may have some weaknesses but she's a great friend. She's loyal. She's dedicated. Write that down. Look at the list every day. Begin to focus on that person's good qualities.

If you're negative toward another person and you operate from a critical spirit it's going to change your attitude toward them and eventually damage that relationship.

Everyone has faults and does things that get on people's nerves. But be careful that you aren't only magnifying the wrong things, because that's how you feed the critical spirit and that's when you start complaining that the wrong egg got fried.

It gets dangerous when, by giving life to negativity, your critique injures someone's self-esteem or discourages them. We've all been on the receiving end and that's no fun; it can damage a relationship and it doesn't feel good. God has called you to lift others up. Your words carry tremendous power. You can use them to build up or use them to tear down. I encourage you to build a life you can be proud of by using your words for the good of others and yourself.

You can't stop all the negative thoughts you'll have about people and situations, but you can stop letting those thoughts create a negative atmosphere by speaking them out loud. I heard it said, "You can't keep the birds from flying over your head, but you can stop them from building a nest in your hair." The choice is ours. We can control what comes out of our mouth.

Before you speak, first step back and remind yourself that complaining only finds the worst in situations and never the best. It doesn't change anything or anyone. Try to see the good in every person or situation rather than giving life to negativity. Don't ruin relationships and experiences. You're never going to see the change you want in yourself or others by finding fault. That will only limit your ability to experience the fullness of what God wants for you.

"So in everything, do to others what you would have them do to you, for this sums up the Law and the Prophets."

—MATTHEW 7:12 NIV

Even if you're the one looking for something different in your relationship today or desperate for change in a situation, ask God to give you the wisdom and strength to be the change you want to see. You can model change for those around you. You can't always make people change, but you can lead the way. You carry seeds of change; if you want more encouragement in your home, be the encourager. If you want more love and affection in your life, show that tender care to those around you. Give your spouse or the people in your life something to draw from. Relationships are just as much about what you give as what you are hoping to receive. When you adjust your attitude, it will create an atmosphere for a positive change.

. . . .

Heavenly Father,

I don't want to miss out on the beauty in my life by seeing what is wrong. I want to be a person who can find the good in people as well as difficult situations. Help me be a problem solver, not a faultfinder. I want to create an atmosphere with my life that helps people to rise higher. I know You will help me see positive change in my life, as well as in the lives of those around me. Thank You for the freedom to do good and enjoy my life.

In Jesus' name,
Amen

· · · · · ● ● ● · · · · ·

Nineteen

Your Ordinary Is Extraordinary

A faithful person will be richly blessed.

PROVERBS 28:20 NIV

Toward the end of Joel's father's life, I would pick him up on Sunday mornings and bring him to church. When we arrived, I would stay with him while a professional hair and makeup artist would get him camera ready to televise the Sunday morning services. One Sunday this woman told Pastor John that it would be her last Sunday because her husband was being relocated for his job. I could tell by my father-in-law's face that he was thinking, *Who are we going to find to replace her by next week?* To my surprise he looked at me and asked, "Victoria, can you do my hair and makeup for TV?" The next thing I knew, without really thinking too much about it, I said, "Sure, I can if you trust me." I wasn't quite qualified— I had no experience with cosmetology other than giving haircuts to a few of my friends in junior high. But that day I got promoted to Top Stylist at Lakewood Church Television Production.

Meanwhile, my cousins in Georgia were planning a big family reunion. They had the venue and the food arranged, they were so excited and had worked so hard to make it a great event. When we spoke on the phone they were giving me all the details and told me I had to be there. I felt bad but I told them that we have services on the weekend and I couldn't be there because I had to do my father-in-law's hair for television. They weren't too happy, and later I found out that they thought my position was not very important and that I had more in me than just doing my father-in-law's hair. I have to admit it hurt my feelings and made me feel like what I was doing was small and unimportant. I had to shake off those feelings and encourage myself to be faithful in what God had me doing right then. It was my chance to do what I had to do with excellence and to the best of my ability.

And that's what I did. I decided that day that I would do his hair better than it had ever been done. For the last years of his life, I was faithful. I picked him up every Sunday and did his hair and makeup to get him ready for the tapings. In my routine, what I didn't realize was that God was preparing me and positioning me for where I am now in ministry. As I was practicing discipline, commitment, and dedication, He was building me, teaching me, and creating something extraordinary through my ordinary days. When I decided to be the best I could right where I was it brought value to my assignment and made great deposits in my life.

Don't let people's opinions of your title or their ideas of

success change your day. Don't let them distract you from what God has called you to do in this time of life. When you see other people's success, victories, or abundance aired on social media, don't let it define how you view your own life right now. Besides, the image of life through social media has been put through a filter. It only represents a fragment of what's really going on in someone's world. Keep your gaze ahead in your own lane, knowing that even though what you're doing might feel ordinary or routine, God is going to turn it into something extraordinary.

We all have times when we ask ourselves, *Is this really what I'm supposed to be doing with my life? Is this even worth it?* That's when we need to remember what the Scripture says, when you are faithful in the small things, God will make you ruler over much. Keep doing what you are doing with excellence and eventually your ordinary will produce extraordinary results. I remember when my children were small I took care of them, watched over them, and changed their diapers. I was faithful to them as a mom. When you have a young family and so many responsibilities to others life can seem so routine and exhausting. It's easy to wonder if they even recognize or appreciate all the labor and attention that goes into them day in and day out. I know that many times I felt like that. However it was in those seemingly ordinary days when I lived life being faithful to my family and to what God had given me to do was how the extraordinary was produced in my life. I can see how those small seeds brought me great joy and abundance. I wouldn't trade anything that I went through to get where I am today.

. . . .

"I came that they may have life and have it abundantly."
—JOHN 10:10 ESV

. . . .

No matter how ordinary it seems, today is a good day. You have an extraordinary life, because it's your life and God gave it to you. He gave you purpose and destiny. You can live fearlessly and freely. Jesus said, "I have come to bring you life and life more abundantly." What does that abundant life look like to you today? Does it look ordinary, boring, or routine? You need to have a mind-set that sees the extraordinary value in what you are doing today. God has given you great assignments that may feel small right now but they are creating and preparing extraordinary blessings in your future. Don't get weary in doing well for you will receive a great harvest at just the right time as you live today in excellence.

. . . .

Heavenly Father,

Thank You for the responsibilities before me today. Help me to do my best in everything, seeing what's extraordinary about where I am now, and knowing You're preparing me for more. I declare that today is a great day.

In Jesus' name,
Amen

· · · · · · ● ● ● · · · · ·

Twenty

Develop Your Potential

No discipline seems pleasant at the time,
but painful. Later on, however,
it produces a harvest of righteousness.

HEBREWS 12:11 NIV

When I was in the fifth grade, I wanted the lead role in our school play, but the teachers didn't choose me. Nevertheless, I imagined that the girl who got the lead wasn't going to be able to play the part, and the teachers would have to pick me after all. I dreamed about it and I enjoyed playing that part in my mind.

I was dreaming about playing the role, but I hadn't actually prepared; I hadn't developed what was inside of me by learning the lines or memorizing the steps. If the teachers had called on me, I wouldn't have been able to play the part because I didn't do what was necessary to develop my ability.

Have you ever felt a stirring inside that tells you that you can do more and rise higher? When you see an opportunity, do you feel excited and really want to go for it? That is your potential—your untapped gifts and talents—calling out to you, saying there is more in you to be developed. You'll just need to make the sacrifice to do what others won't do if you're going to pursue those gifts and callings in your life. It will take time, effort, and determination, but the sacrifice will be worth it.

God doesn't want you to merely sit around dreaming about what you can accomplish. You must put action behind your desires and work toward the goal you have in mind. I heard it said that success happens when preparation meets opportunity. That's why it is important to give it your all and continually develop your gifts. That way, when the right opportunity presents itself, you can walk through the door with confidence.

* *

The path of the righteous is like the morning sun, shining ever brighter till the full light of day.

—PROVERBS 4:18 NIV

* *

You have a deep well of talent inside of you, but the only way to get that talent up and out of you is to develop it. You must be determined to use what you have even if there are obstacles. Sometimes challenges and hard circumstances are what keep us from moving toward our goals. We are afraid of failure or what people might think. Maybe you tried once but it didn't work out. Don't shrink back. You must learn to not focus on the obstacle but your goal. Tap into the potential that is inside of you. To develop that potential takes determination and persistence. The only way you can fail is if you quit. Don't give up. God will help you be fearless as you pursue the desires of your heart if you ask Him for His help.

I heard a story about a hiker who had traveled miles across the desert. His water supply ran out and he knew if he didn't find water soon, he would surely die. He came upon an old rusty well with a tin can tied to the handle. It had a note tucked inside, which read:

Dear Stranger,
This water pump is in working condition but, in order for the water to come out, the pump needs to be primed. I buried a jar of water under the white rock out of the sun. There is enough water to prime the pump, but not if you drink any first. When you are finished, will you please fill the jar and put it back as you found it, for the next stranger who comes this way?

There will be times in life you'll have to be willing to pour everything you have into your dream and give it all you have. And in times you fear you're out of resources, trust that God will help you tap into the deep abundant supply of talent and strength He has given you. Be willing to prime the pump with the determination to give life your all, because God has filled you with everything you need to succeed.

God breathed His life into you and created you to win. When you put actions behind your faith, you'll receive wisdom, strength, and creativity to help you accomplish your dreams and desires. Believe in yourself, because you have what it takes to develop the potential God has placed in you.

. . . .

Heavenly Father,

I don't want to miss the right opportunities because I am not prepared. Today and each day, help me invest in my potential to fearlessly accomplish all You made me for. I am determined to use what I have and believe that You will develop me into more. Thank You for helping me recognize what I am good at and what path to pursue. I declare that I am well-able and free to do what You have called me to do.

In Jesus' name,
Amen

Twenty-One

Your Gift Back to God

Let all that I am praise the LORD; may I never forget the good things he does for me.

PSALM 103:2 NLT

When I was in the second grade I became extremely ill. My mother took me back and forth to the doctor for over a week before I was admitted to the hospital. Because I couldn't hold down food, I was getting weaker and weaker. For six weeks the doctors examined my blood so they could try to figure out what was wrong. I had so many IVs in my arms that they became stiff and painful. My mom would stay with me during the day and my dad would stay all night. It was a scary time for my family. The doctors eventually diagnosed me and were able to treat me with the right medication.

Two months later I was well enough and had the strength to go back to school. During that time my dad would always say to me, "When you get well, I will buy you anything you want." That was my dad's way of getting my mind off of the hospital stay and onto the future. When I was well I held Dad to his promise. That's when he took me and bought me the desire of my heart: an apricot toy poodle that I named Jo Jo.

I will never forget that it was God who gave the doctors the ability to find the right medicines that led to my healing. It was God who gave me a family who loved me and took such good care of me. When I look back over my life and recall all God has done, an overwhelming sense of gratitude stirs my heart to not only live with passion and purpose, but to ask myself what I can possibly do to pay the Lord back for all his kindness toward me.

I know you are like me and you, too, can think of so many things the Lord has done for you. Every one of us has seen God's goodness and mercy in our lives. He has made ways where it didn't seem there could ever be a way. He has given us promotions and has brought the right people into our lives. He has taken care of our families and brought us through challenges that were overwhelming and difficult. Our lives should be so stirred with such gratitude that we ask the question, "How can I give back to such a great God?"

King David in the Bible felt the same way. He was so moved in his heart with gratitude as he recalled all of God's goodness toward him. The cry of his heart is recorded in the Psalms.

. . . .

What can I offer to the LORD for all he has done for me?

—PSALM 116:12 NLT

. . . .

David was so full of gratitude as he recalled that it was God who had brought him through his battles and helped him overcome giants that he couldn't help but ask, "How can I repay God for His blessings?"

Have you ever felt so blessed you wanted to repay God? I know I have. We could never repay God for what He has done. Salvation is free for us. "For it is by grace you have been saved, through faith—and this is a gift from God." It is not a one-time gift, but a gift that keeps on giving. A gift that gives us health, prosperity, wholeness, redemption, and protection. These are some of the promises that we can hold on to. Our best gift we can give back to God is to take hold of His great promises and to live fearlessly and freely.

David felt an overwhelming desire to honor God with his life, so the question he asked in Psalm 116:12 he answers in the next verse: "I will take up the cup of salvation and call upon his name" (Psalms 116:13, NLT). David meant that he would simply receive all God had for him. He accepted God's deliverance and honored Him by continually calling upon His name. Even though David made many mistakes, he never stopped going back to God to receive God's much-needed gift of grace for his life.

If we would only receive what the Lord has done for us, even when we don't feel worthy, we would find ourselves moving forward instead of getting stuck. We should always go to God, even on our worst days, because God only desires to give us His best. His ears are always open to a heart that is willing to sing in His presence no matter what circumstances we find ourselves in.

We should never shy away from our salvation. Salvation isn't just about eternity; it's about how we live now and how we show honor to God, knowing that we have been delivered and set free from a life of guilt and condemnation. Our gift back to God is to represent His goodness here on earth and shout our thanks to the world for what He has done for us. Take hold of what Jesus did for you. Don't shrink back in fear and allow your past to dictate your future. You have so much more in store for you. Step into your position as a child of the King and move forward in faith, fearlessly and freely. That's the gift that God loves.

. . . .

Heavenly Father,
Thank You for all the wonderful gifts You have given me. I will take <u>hold</u> of Your grace and move forward

love mercy

in faith, knowing the greatest gift I can give back to You is to get up and boldly receive what You have done for me. I will call upon You in all I do and know that You are always here to give me what I need. I will shake off my mistakes and take up Your strength as I walk into the salvation You have already given to me.

In Jesus' name,
Amen

Twenty-Two

. . . . ● ● ● . . . .

Release It to God

"Whoever tries to keep their life will lose it,
and whoever loses their life will preserve it."

LUKE 17:32–33 NIV

Hunters used to trap monkeys by filling a large barrel with bananas and then cutting a small hole in the side of it, just big enough for the monkey to put his hand and arm through. The monkey, completely unaware of the trap, would reach his arm into the barrel and grab one of those bananas. But when he tried to pull his arm out he wouldn't be able to get both his clenched fist and the banana back through the small hole. The monkey could easily let go of the banana and pull his hand out of the barrel, but the monkey wanted the banana so badly that he wouldn't release it from his hand; therefore the hunters could easily capture the monkey.

You will keep in perfect peace those whose minds are steadfast, because they trust in you.

—ISAIAH 26:3 NIV

Sometimes, we can be a bit like the monkey. We want something so badly that we fall into the trap of holding on tightly, and it keeps us from the new things God wants to do in our lives. Don't get trapped because you aren't willing to change or reposition yourself or your thinking. God always has your best in mind. His plans are for your good, and when you follow His plans, you can move forward in the freedom and victory he has for you. Letting go is not always easy. It can be letting go of wrong mindsets or attitudes. It can be letting go of questions about something that didn't work out, or letting go of an old relationship. Don't hold on to anything you know you should release. Let it go so God can give you something better. Trust in God and He will give you peace about your decision.

Many times, I have had to give up my plan and my desires to adjust myself to what God was doing in my life. When God called Joel and me into the ministry there were so many adjustments to make. Life got a bit more hectic and complicated. I had to adapt to this new way of doing things and reposition my life for full-time ministry. It wasn't always easy to let go of the way things used to be. But during the process God always gave me something more fulfilling. I can look back now, even at the times when I didn't fully understand where things were going for us, and say, "I am glad I didn't get trapped in the old life."

Just like me, you may not always understand the changes happening in your life while you're living them in the moment, but that's when you have to trust God's goodness and believe He is freeing you into bigger and better things. Today, be open-handed, open-minded, and open-hearted to what God has for you.

. . . .

Heavenly Father,
Today I let go of anything that is trying to keep me trapped, whether it is wrong mind-sets, attitudes, or friendships. I release my life to You because I believe that when You close one door, You will open up a better door. I am willing to adjust my life so that I live in step with Your plans. Thank You for guiding me and leading me into a bright future.

In Jesus' name,
Amen

· · · · · ● ● ● · · · ·

Twenty-Three

Know Your Big Brother

"For whoever does the will of My Father in heaven is My brother and sister and mother."

MATTHEW 12:50 NKJV

There's something wonderful about having a good big brother. I am fortunate to have one. Yes, when we were growing up, he would tickle me until I almost wet my pants. He wouldn't let me play with his most prized toys, and he always jumped on my bike when I was about to ride it. Then he would give it back after he'd had a good laugh. One thing I knew about my big brother, though, was that he loved me. He would show me in many different ways. He was always the one who would shield me when the bullies showed up. He's the one who had my back and would always take up for me. He was a great example and helped me get further in life than I would have on my own.

As good as he was, he couldn't do what my big brother Jesus has done for me.

Like the best of big brothers, Jesus defends us and fights our battles for us. He stands between the enemy and us. He is constantly pleading our case and taking up for us. He shows us how to live and leads us along the best paths.

You may not have had a good big brother growing up. You may have even thought *I wish I had a different family*, but with Jesus as your big brother, you have the same DNA as Heaven. God is your Father and Heaven is cheering you on.

With Jesus you have a big brother that sticks by your side through thick and thin. Because He overcame everything that was against Him, He will help you overcome the difficulties you face. You can always count on him. Call out to your big brother Jesus today; He wants to help you in every way. Be confident that when the bullies come out you are not alone. You can tell those circumstances that are trying to bully you, "I may look small, but I've got a big brother that can whup you." Tell the enemy of doubt and fear, "If you mess with me, you mess with my big brother, so you need to go."

. . . .

Both the one who makes people holy and those who are made holy are of the same family. So Jesus is not ashamed to call them brothers and sisters.

—HEBREWS 2:11 NIV

. . . .

Don't get too far away from your big brother. Stay close to Him. Don't walk too far ahead or get distracted by the wrong things and fall behind. Keep your eyes on Him. Learn from Him. And if you fall and get hurt, remember that your big brother is strong enough to carry you. You are protected, and you are loved. Stay under the shadow of your big brother and let Him fight your battles for you.

. . . .

Heavenly Father,

Thank You that I am in the family of God through Your son, Jesus. I will call on the name of Jesus, and He will be with me at all times. I will not be afraid because my big brother Jesus is fighting my battles and He is strong enough to take care of me, no matter what is coming against me. I will walk fearlessly in freedom from my troubles, knowing that Jesus is by my side and helping me. Thank you, Jesus, for overcoming and for giving me Your name that overcomes the world.

In Jesus' name,
Amen

· · · · · ● ● ● · · · ·

Twenty-Four

Don't Block
the SON

*In the same way, let your light shine before
others, that they may see your good deeds
and glorify your Father in heaven.*

MATTHEW 5:16 NIV

Not long ago, I was browsing in a local garden store when I discovered these beautiful solar-powered path lights, and they were on sale. So of course I bought them, and when I got home I found the perfect spot for them, right beside the steps off of our back porch. It was a bright, sunny afternoon, so I fully expected my new little lights would be charged by nightfall. I was excited about my purchase and could hardly wait to show Joel. After dinner, Joel and I went for a walk, and when we came around the corner toward the back porch, I thought I'd see a warm glow coming from the new lights. But you know what I saw? Nothing. Not even a dim flicker. I was a little frustrated, but I was hopeful the lights just needed another day in the sun to power up.

The next night, Joel and I went out for our evening walk, and as we headed toward the back porch the walkway was still dark. By this time, I was really annoyed. I thought, *No wonder these lights were on sale. They don't work.* I bent down and pulled the first light out of the ground, fully intending to return the lights to the garden store. But as I lifted the light up, I noticed a tiny little tab that said, "Pull." I hadn't seen that before, but those tabs were on every single light. I pulled every tab, and the next night, those lights were shining brightly. They were beautiful.

- -

"Children of God"... you will shine among them like stars in the sky.

—PHILIPPIANS 2:15 NIV

- -

You know, we're a lot like those sun-powered lights. We can be in the presence of the powerful light of the S-O-N all day long, but if there's something blocking us, we won't ever receive His power and we won't ever shine. We have to "pull the tab," so to speak, on doubt, fear, bitterness, negativity, anger, and forgiveness, and to remove anything that might prevent us from powering up in the Son's presence. We have to open our hearts to Him so that we can reflect His light to the world. You see, we have the seed of God inside of us. When we bask in His presence we are illuminated, just as God designed. The Scriptures say we are meant to shine like stars in the universe, so let me ask you this—is there anything blocking you from the S-O-N today?

It's not always bad things that block us from receiving from God. Sometimes busyness or even overcommitment to good things can keep us from reading God's Word and spending time in the light of His presence. When that happens, we need to cut out some of those activities and withdraw from excessive commitments that are crowding our lives. We must do whatever it takes to spend time in His light.

I saw this truth play out in nature not long ago. We have a pretty big tree in our backyard that had me puzzled because it was growing at such an odd angle. I thought, *That is so weird. I wonder why it grows that way.* One day, when I was talking with our landscaper, I asked him about it. He explained, "It grows at a slant because so many shrubs and other trees around it are crowding out the light. That tree is struggling to grow toward the light. If you'll prune away some of the bushes and branches, you'll make room for the light to get to that tree, and it may just straighten up and grow properly."

Maybe you've let too many things crowd your life. Or perhaps you've allowed friends who don't share your same values to overshadow you. No matter the cause, I encourage you to prune your life of whatever is stopping you from being fully exposed to God. Ask Him to help you get rid of any unneeded busyness and call on Him to free you from any fear, anger, bitterness, or forgiveness in your heart. Begin weeding out those friends who keep you in a dark place and commit today that you won't let anything or anyone keep you from spending time with God. If you'll do these things, you'll walk fearlessly and freely in the Light, and you'll become the bright reflection He designed you to be.

. . . .

Heavenly Father,

Search me, God, and if there is anything in the way of Your light shining on me and in me, please remove it from my life. Help me not to get too busy or allow others to steal my time with You. Uproot any discouragement, bitterness, unforgiveness, or anger from my heart, Father, and let it never return again. I desire to be a bright light in this world, shining Your love onto everyone I encounter. I love you, Lord.

In Jesus' name,

Amen

· · · · · ● ● ● · · ·

Twenty-Five

Don't Give Life to Negativity

Do all things without grumbling
and faultfinding and complaining.

PHILIPPIANS 2:14 AMPC

Why do we complain? We're all guilty of it, but why do we complain so easily? I think it's mostly because we need to get something off our chest. When we don't like what the boss wants us to do, when there's something at church we think could be better, or when someone does or says something that bothers us, it just feels good to vent. We might also think that if we complain enough about a situation or what a person is doing, we can bring change. But that only makes the situation worse. When we give life to our negative thoughts by speaking them, we create a negative environment and that negativity pollutes and spreads to those around us.

Complaining is not as harmless as we might think. Many studies have researched the effects of complaining on the brain. When we complain, we rewire or retrain our brain. Our brain wants to take the path of least resistance, so it wants to repeat a pattern. When we complain, we learn to complain more. If we're not careful, we set our brain in a negative thought pattern that's tough to revert.

Today you're going to have many opportunities to complain because there's no perfect friend, no perfect spouse, no perfect child, and no perfect job. Life is filled with imperfections, so we can't escape the fact that there will be much to criticize. Instead of complaining, we can be intentional to positively respond to the negative feelings and thoughts we inevitably have—first, by training our brain to see God and how He can work in these situations.

- -

Finally, brothers and sisters, whatever is true, whatever is noble, whatever is right, whatever is pure, whatever is lovely, whatever is admirable—if anything is excellent or praiseworthy—think about such things.

—PHILIPPIANS 4:8 NIV

- -

The apostle Paul said that what we nurture on the inside is what's going to come through on the outside. God wants us to train our thoughts on what is good so we don't give life to negativity.

In the Scriptures, this is seen clearly when God brought the people of Israel out of slavery in Egypt. Having been mistreated for so long, they were filled with negativity, which God wanted to replace in them with thoughts of victory. So as they left Egypt, God had the Egyptians pour out their abundant wealth on His people—gold and silver and cattle. When they got to the Red Sea, He parted the water so they walked through on dry land and delivered them from Pharaoh's army. This was followed by one miracle after another. But as they went on their way, they soon started seeing things they thought could be better and began to complain and grumble. First it was about Moses' leadership, then about their food, water, and other conditions. Their number one enemy was their own complaining, which gave life to negativity that slowed down their progress. What should have been an eleven-day journey into the Promised Land took them forty years.

The Israelites never trained their brains to *not* complain, and they got stuck in the wilderness. Have you ever thought that your own grumbling and complaining could literally stop you from going to the next level—to a job promotion, to a healthy marriage, to a deeper relationship with God? Have you ever thought about how unhealthy negativity really is? Here's the good news: If your mind can be trained to complain, then your mind can be trained to find the best. When we learn to look for what is good it brings strength and encouragement to our hearts. It can bring peace and joy even in the difficult situations.

The Bible says that when the Israelites were complaining about their situation, it was the same as complaining about God. They limited their faith in Him and didn't trust Him to fulfill their needs. But just like the Israelites, God has already given you everything you need to get where you're going. God made you to be more than a conqueror, and to be an overcomer. He knows you'll face challenges, but He wants you to train your mind to trust Him to lead you to the fullness of your destiny.

The next time you see a situation or a loved one that makes you want to complain, don't give a place to those negative thoughts by speaking them. Complaining doesn't change anything, it only makes things worse. It can ruin a relationship and limit what God wants to do in your life. That doesn't have to be you.

God is leading you as He did the Israelites. Remember not to weaken your faith by complaining, but to strengthen your faith by seeing the good on your journey. You can train your mind to see God and how He can work in every situation.

. . . .

Heavenly Father,

I know today I'll have negative thoughts, but I won't give them life by complaining. Help me instead to be positive and to see the ways You meet my needs. I will put a guard over my lips and trust You to guide me in all my ways. Thank You for self-control and the discipline to see the blessings that are in my life today.

In Jesus' name,

Amen

Twenty-Six

Be Intentional with Your Time

*Be very careful, then, how you live—
not as unwise but as wise, making the most
of every opportunity...*

EPHESIANS 5:15–16 NIV

It is always interesting how we prepare ourselves for a New Year. Our expectation is high, so we set out to improve our lives in many areas. We gear up to eat right, exercise, and use our time to the fullest. One New Year, all my friends were setting themselves up to conquer the year by establishing their "word" for the year. That sounded like a good idea, so I thought of what my "word" could be. I really gave it my time and attention and the word *intentional* came to my mind. After all, don't we all want to live an intentional life? We have desires, dreams, and hopes for a better way of doing things.

When my friends asked me what my word for the year was, I proudly said, "Intentional." But it didn't take me long to realize that *good intentions* aren't enough. Although it sounded good, I saw how many things I did out of habit and still found myself taking longer to accomplish my daily goals, because other things in my day easily distracted me. It's so easy in the morning to pick up our phones and look at our text messages, scan our emails, check out social media, or scroll the news feed, and before we know it, a lot of time has gotten away from us. Meanwhile, many of us rush through breakfast or take it on the run; we barely engage our families in the mornings. We find ourselves missing great opportunities to spend time in a more valuable way. Because we spend time with less important activities, we rush to accomplish the things that we want to achieve.

If we are going to reach our goals, we have to set a plan *on purpose* and take an action. In fact, the word *intention* means an aim or a plan. It isn't just about setting goals; it's about setting a plan to reach those goals. If we are going to live fearlessly and freely, we need to be more interested in reaching our goal than just merely setting our goal.

* * *

The plans of the diligent lead to profit as surely as haste leads to poverty.

—PROVERBS 21:5 NIV

* * *

You have heard the old saying, "There is only one way to eat an elephant—one bite at a time." That means that when we are trying to accomplish a goal that we haven't achieved in the past or that seems impossible, the only way to conquer it is a little at a time. There have been studies that say we are capable of far more than we realize. We just need to manage our time and harness our energy. I had to learn this, as I became aware that if my intentions are going to become a reality, setting time-bound goals will help me to achieve my intentions.

It is so easy to become distracted, waste precious time, and look up to realize that our day has gone by and we have not achieved what we would have liked to. When it comes to time, we're all on equal playing fields. We all have 1,440 minutes each and every day; however, many of us differ in the way we choose to utilize those minutes. I am blessed to have in my life a husband that has a great concept of and respect for time. He knows how to use it to his advantage. He always reminds me, "Time is such a precious commodity; it's something that we can't make any more of." Material things can always be replaced or replenished, but we will never get this day back. How we choose to spend our time is personal and unique to all of us. My personality is different from Joel's. My responsibilities and the way I carry out my assignments look different and require different giftings. But one thing I know for certain, time is worth being managed because we are only allotted so much.

We need to be intentional with our time, knowing

that ultimately, many of the fleeting things that capture our attention are not going to matter.

If you're going to experience the best of what God has in store for you, you'll have to prioritize your time by doing what matters most in your life. Busyness won't get you where you want to go but spending your time with focused intent will. Whatever you want to accomplish is possible when you take time to cultivate it. I am still learning to be much more intentional when it comes to time because intention is an action that must always be exercised. I am passionate about changing patterns in my life and growing more in my time management. Whether it is to accomplish my dreams or simply take time to relax or be with my family, I am conscious of the importance of using it wisely. One thing that has helped me is to set timers for my activities. When I exercise, I allot a certain amount of time so I will have an awareness and make the most of my time regardless if it is spent in the gym or walking in the neighborhood. You can't always live by a timer, but I encourage you to be intentional in the areas you want to improve and spend your time wisely in those areas. It's not about counting the minutes but making the minutes count.

. . . .

Heavenly Father,

You have given me this day and I want to set my intentions on accomplishing what will move me closer to my dreams and hopes for the future. Help me to use my time wisely, and to choose the activities that will bring honor to You and enrich my life. Help me to not rush through the important areas and waste time on unnecessary distractions. I want to live with good intentions that put action behind my faith. Thank You for all that You have given me and for helping me in all that I do.

In Jesus' name,
Amen

Twenty-Seven

• • • • • ● • ● • • • • •

A Fresh
Perspective

Always be joyful. Never stop praying.
Be thankful in all circumstances, for this
is God's will for you who belong to Christ Jesus.

1 THESSALONIANS 5:16–18 NLT

I heard a funny anecdote about a young athlete who accidentally lost one of her contact lenses on the soccer field during the biggest game of the year. As one of the team's star players, it was a real problem that she couldn't see well, because that meant she also couldn't play well. After crawling around on her hands and knees, searching for the lens for what seemed like hours without success, her mom bounded onto the field, dropped to the grass, and began searching for that contact lens. Just moments later, the determined mom announced, "I found it," holding up the lens for all to see. The daughter was thrilled but puzzled. She said, "Mom, I looked everywhere. How in the world did you find my contact lens?" Her mom replied, "Honey, you were looking for a contact lens in the grass, but I was looking for $150."

It's all about perspective, isn't it? Sure, it was important to the daughter that she find her contact lens, but it was even more important to her mom because she was the one who'd originally paid for it. Mama was pursuing that $150 contact lens with great passion. You see, perspective affects how we go about everything we do. It colors how we view our circumstances. The right perspective can make you try harder, be braver, and go for your dreams. However, the wrong perspective can make you settle for less than your best, or worse, become your own worst enemy.

If you're a baseball fan, you've probably heard of the late great pitcher José Lima. He gained a reputation for greatness as a starting pitcher for the Houston Astros in the late 1990s. This young, talented pitcher learned about the power of perspective the hard way. When the Astros built their new stadium, the fence in left field was much closer than it had been in the Astrodome. In fact, the stadium has one of the shortest distances from home plate to the left-field fence than any baseball park in the entire country. This, of course, benefits the hitter, not the pitcher, and Lima couldn't get over that fact. He was overheard saying, "I'll never be able to pitch in here." Turns out, he was right. He had the worst season of his career. He went from being a twenty-game winner to a sixteen-game loser in back-to-back seasons. See, José Lima allowed the wrong perspective to dominate his thoughts, and then he gave birth to that defeat when he spoke them aloud.

If we're going to experience God's best in our lives, we need to start fresh with a positive perspective. The Bible says we can do all things through Christ Who gives us strength, and it gives us an example of right perspective when we take that into account. Basically, knowing that

Christ is our strength and sustainer should give us an outlook of victory, prosperity, and security. We don't have to fear not having enough or measuring up; we don't have to darken our perspective by comparing what we have with what somebody else has. We have it all in Christ alone, and that gift is equally real and accessible to every person on earth who wants to claim it. In other words, we have everything we need to succeed.

. . . .

No, in all these things we are more than conquerors through him who loved us.

—ROMANS 8:37 NIV

. . . .

It can be hard to have a perspective of success if you're feeling overwhelmed and defeated due to negative circumstances, but you can do it. You can choose to have the right perspective; it'll just take work. Every day, you get to choose what kind of attitude you're going to have. You can look on the bright side, expect good things, and believe that your dreams will come to pass, or you can choose to be negative, focus on your problems, dwell on what didn't work out, and live worried and discouraged.

It's a choice that we all make every single day. Life will go so much better if you will simply choose to have a positive perspective. When you wake up in the morning, choose to be happy. Choose to be grateful for the day. Choose to focus on your possibilities.

I know a man who experienced a major perspective shift when he was diagnosed with cancer. His road to recovery was long and hard, but he told me that during his battle, he started focusing more on his family and friends and less on his career. He didn't let the stress of his job get to him anymore or rule his thoughts. He also learned that the notion of a bucket list was useless to him. When he was sick, he could have cared less about having experiences he'd never had—what he wanted was more of the same—more time just being in his family's company. He got a new appreciation for life through his changed perspective.

Always be joyful. Never stop praying. Be thankful in all circumstances, for this is God's will for you who belong to Christ Jesus.

—1 THESSALONIANS 5:16–18 NLT

You can make the best out of any circumstance. Even a terrible health diagnosis can produce positive changes in a person's life, as long as that person has the right perspective. Part of choosing to have a positive perspective is simply having a grateful heart. I recommend you make a list today of what you have to be thankful for. Make another list of past experiences that have been pivotal for you at various stages of life—the jobs you've had, the homes you've lived in, your important relationships, anything—and see how far God has brought you. Let me assure you, He's just getting started! You see, it's a waste of time to think about what you don't have and what you haven't yet done, when you can enjoy what's yours now and what God is doing in your life today. Don't spend your life worried about what might happen. Spend your days in divine expectation of all that God has for you.

. . . .

Heavenly Father,
I praise You for how much You've given me and how far You've brought me in life.

It's easy to forget or be distracted from my blessings today when I compare myself with others or lose perspective on what I have. Help me to gain a new appreciation for the gifts in my life and help me to choose to have the right perspective in every circumstance.

In Jesus' name,
Amen

Twenty–Eight

Don't Fall into the Comparison Trap

*Therefore, since we are surrounded by such
a great cloud of witnesses, let us throw off
everything that hinders and the sin that so easily
entangles. And let us run with perseverance
the race marked out for us.*

HEBREWS 12:1 NIV

One day, a friend was at our house with his young son, Denver, who was out playing in our backyard. It was a few days after Easter and, as he explored the area, he found three plastic eggs left over from our annual family Easter brunch. As you can imagine, he was really excited to discover the contents of those three eggs, so he quickly opened them, one right after the other. When he was done, he had two fists full of candy and a huge smile on his face. There was only one problem—it was dinnertime and I didn't want to send him home to his momma full of sugar. Before he could even unwrap that first piece, I said, "Denver, let's go inside and see what other snacks we can find in the pantry."

As I was pointing out other snacks in the pantry, his eyes landed on a basket that was chock-full of different types of candies.

"Could I see *that* basket?" he asked.

I said, "Denver, you already have candy."

He said, "I know, but I see some candy that I like better than what I have."

Suddenly, the candy he'd emptied from the Easter eggs just moments before didn't seem nearly as exciting. He wasn't sure he had the *right* candy or the *best* candy when he saw all of the other options. Denver had fallen victim to the comparison trap, as so many of us do in today's world. When he compared his three eggs full of candy to the huge basket of candy, suddenly his candy didn't seem so special. All the excitement of finding those eggs full of candy went out the window when he saw something that he thought looked better than what he had.

We have all been tempted to fall into the trap of comparison; we see something that looks better than what we have and it makes us feel like we are lacking in some way.

If you spend much time on social media, it's easy to fall prey to the comparison trap. You see people taking elaborate vacations, and you haven't taken a trip in ten years. Or, one of your friends posts pictures of her new car, and you're still driving an old model that you bought from a friend. Maybe your coworker shares about their recent promotion, and that feeling of not being smart enough or good enough begins to fill your mind. When you begin to think in terms of comparison it can cause you to doubt yourself. You may question your ability, your looks, or you may think, *Do I have a good personality; am I clever enough for people to like me?*

When the wrong thoughts fill our minds it can make us shrink back. No one increases in confidence by spending their time thinking about what they don't have.

Comparison is a thief that would like to rob us of our self-worth and take the joy of who we are and what we are becoming right out of our life. You might be happy in your current job until you see someone else's position is more prestigious. The job that you were happy with suddenly seems unimportant because your focus changed and you began to compare.

I had a friend who asked me to go to a home show to get ideas on how to update her cute fixer-upper, but when she saw all of the luxurious home décor and new appliances, she lost her appreciation for the house she had been so excited to redo. She became overwhelmed with the idea that her home would never look as good as all the displays she was seeing. Instead of being grateful for what she had and using her ability to make her home unique and personal to her style, she was losing her vision for what it could become. She was comparing the amenities in her house with all that was featured at the event. This can happen with your job, with your house, with your car, with your family…with your life.

Like Denver, comparison can cause you to not appreciate what is in your hands right now and to long for what you don't have. Instead of enjoying and using what you have you will be thinking *if only I could have the candy in that basket*. Don't lose the joy and satisfaction of what you have because you are comparing it to something else. The Scriptures tell us to run our own race, keep our eyes on our own life and what God has given us. Don't be lured into comparing yourself, your job, your children, or your spouse with anything or anyone. There is no comparison. No one is like you or ever will be.

- -

Each one should test their own actions. Then they can take pride in themselves alone, without comparing themselves to someone else, for each one should carry their own load.
—GALATIANS 6:4–5 NIV

- -

You are unique in every way. Even your fingerprint is one of a kind. There is no one in the universe with it. You have been designed and equipped with everything you need to become all you were created to be. If you want to improve your life you must understand that you aren't lacking but you have the ability to rise higher and advance from right where you are and with what you have. Stay in your lane and run your own race.

God has a unique plan for your life; don't waste your

time looking at what someone else has and become discouraged. I have heard it said, "Count your blessings and not the blessings of someone else." Learn to be grateful for what you have and to celebrate with others what they have been given. If you'll focus on what you *do* have, and you'll tend to it, making the most of it, God will bless it and multiply it. When we do this, we can sidestep the comparison trap and live in the freedom to enjoy what we have and where we are going.

. . . .

Heavenly Father,

Help me to run my race without getting caught up in the comparison trap. You are a good God and I'm thankful for the many blessings in my life. It's my desire to maintain a grateful heart and stop comparing my life to other people's lives, knowing that You have a good plan for me, and that there are more than enough blessings to go around. When I start to get my eyes off of You, Lord, please help me to reset my focus so that I can walk confidently in my calling with a joyful heart and a peaceful spirit.

In Jesus' name,
Amen

· · · · · ● ● ● · · · ·

Twenty-Nine

Let God Multiply What's in Your Hands

*"Truly I tell you, if you have faith as small as
a mustard seed, you can say to this mountain,
'Move from here to there,' and it will move.
Nothing will be impossible for you."*

MATTHEW 17:20 NIV

Jesus was teaching a large crowd of people in a remote area and it became late in the day. The disciples, knowing that the people were getting hungry, suggested that Jesus send the people off to the villages so they could buy food for themselves.

> As evening approached, the disciples came to him and said, "This is a remote place, and it's already getting late. Send the crowds away, so they can go to the villages and buy themselves some food." Jesus replied, "They do not need to go away. You give them something to eat." "We have here only five loaves of bread and two fish," they answered. "Bring them here to me," he said. (Matthew 14:15–18 NIV)

Jesus issued a challenge to the disciples, telling them to feed the people. I am sure they thought there was no way they could feed them all; they only had five loaves of bread and two fish—not nearly enough to feed the huge crowd. Jesus instructed them to bring what they had to Him.

The Bible says that Jesus took the five loaves and two fish and, looking up to the heavens, He gave thanks for what He had and then broke the loaves. Notice, He gave thanks for what He had even when it didn't look like it was enough to meet the present need. As He began giving food to His disciples to distribute to the people, it was multiplied; they fed over 5,000 men plus women and children, and the Scripture says they all ate and were satisfied. Instead of complaining and looking at the lack, He chose to be grateful. Giving thanks started the miracle of multiplication.

* * *

He directed the people to sit down on the grass. Taking the five loaves and the two fish and looking up to heaven, he gave thanks and broke the loaves. Then he gave them to the disciples, and the disciples gave them to the people. They all ate and were satisfied, and the disciples picked up twelve basketfuls of broken pieces that were left over. The number of those who ate was about five thousand men, besides women and children.

—MATTHEW 14:19–21 NIV

* * *

Jesus showed us that we should put what we don't think is enough into God's hands. Don't complain; don't give up. Give thanks for what you do have. Show God that you recognize you have something. When you have the attitude of thankfulness, God can breathe in your direction and multiply it. The suggestion to dismiss the people was the easy way out. When you have the attitude of "not enough," you may reject the idea of doing something great in your life. Do you have something in your heart, but you don't feel like you have the resources, the education, the time, or the ability to see it through? It's easy to dismiss the idea and send it away. Don't let what you think is *not enough* keep you from a miracle in your life.

The disciples had something for God to work with. When you recognize you have something, even if it doesn't look like much in comparison to what you need, that's the start. Get up every day and use what's in your hands. What you may think is small has tremendous potential when you put it in God's hands. Don't dismiss the ordinary in your life. God can use the ordinary to do extraordinary miracles. Hold each day up to God and give thanks, using what is in your hands, and watch God fulfill your dreams and bring you peace, joy, and satisfaction.

. . . .

Heavenly Father,

I thank You that Jesus showed me how to bring You my dreams, gifts, and talent. I place all that concerns me into Your hands and I give You thanks for what You have given me, even when I can't see how it can multiply to cover my needs. I believe You are the God of multiplication. I will commit to use what is available to me today. And You will provide what is needed to bring about the miracle. Thank You for all that You have given me and all You are going to do in my life.

In Jesus' Name,
Amen

Thirty

Patience Under Construction

Be still before the LORD
and wait patiently for him.

PSALM 37:7 NIV

If you've ever been around a construction site—where a building is going up or where changes are being made to the highways—you know it can be messy, and the process can seem to take forever. Years ago, when Joel and I were building our house, I would go to the site on a regular basis and check the progress in the different phases of construction. Each time I'd think to myself, *I don't like this—it's moving too slowly. I want to see more progress.*

One time before the roof was on there was a big storm and it rained hard for several days. After the rain stopped we went over to check on the house. Mud had been tracked through the house. Water was puddled in lower areas, and the trash hadn't been picked up because of the rain. It was disorganized and messy. I was so impatient and frustrated I felt like saying, "This is never going to be what it should be." But, of course I didn't. Even though it looked like a disaster that was never going to be finished, I knew it was part of the process and it would take time.

In the same way, you have to see the things that are messy, the things you struggle with, and the things that seem out of place in your life, as simply being under construction. This doesn't mean it's not going to work out. That water in your living room, the muddy floor, the disappointment, the betrayal, the delay—you may not like these things but they're all a part of the process. You're under construction. You can't become all you were created to be without some messy places. To the untrained eye, a construction site can look disorganized and random, but to the architect it's no big deal. They're not worried. They drew the plans. They know exactly where it's going. Your architect is the Most High God. He's designed a specific plan for your life.

. . . .

For we are God's masterpiece. He has created us anew in Christ Jesus, so we can do the good things he planned for us long ago.

—EPHESIANS 2:10 NLT

. . . .

There's a common saying that goes, "I'm not who I want to be, but thank God I'm not who I used to be." I love that because it reminds me how we're all under construction. We are all works in progress. Right now, God is busy making each one of us into who He wants us to be, and that's a good thing. Just as Philippians 1:6 promises, God is not going to quit in the middle of the job. He's not going to stop His work until He completes us. We have to hold on to that promise and be patient for the result in His time, knowing it'll be worth the wait.

Paul said in Ephesians that you are "a masterpiece." You may not be there quite yet, but instead of living with the negative recording in your mind that says you don't measure up, or beating yourself up for the mistakes you have made, change your attitude to say, "I'm a masterpiece in the making. I may be struggling in some areas, but I know a secret. God is still working on me. I'm under construction. I'm better than I was last year. I'm growing. I'm coming up higher and I know this: what God started, He's going to finish." You have to look beyond the mess and see the masterpiece.

Having faith in God, and in His promise to finish the work He has begun, will give you the patience needed to not only survive but thrive during every phase of your construction. And when it moves more slowly than you expected, or it seems quiet, like nothing is happening, just know that God is still with you, making you. He's at work, creating the best version of who you can become. But you have to trust Him in the process, because there will be some phases when things don't look good. You'll think, *This isn't at all what I envisioned.* That's when you have to see yourself through God's eyes. While your life might not look great through your natural eyes during this phase, remember that you're under construction. What looks like a hot mess today will be beautiful when God is finished. Someday, you'll look back over the various stages of construction and understand the need for each one and why each stage took so long. So, in the moments when you're tempted to be impatient with the process, you can remember God's promise to finish what He started and wait for Him with joy and expectation.

. . . .

Heavenly Father,

When I'm discouraged by my circumstances or impatient with my progress, I will hold on to the promise of Philippians 1:6, that You will not stop before completing me. I will look for joy in every phase of construction, knowing that as I look to You, the architect of my life, I will continue to become all I was intended to be. I believe I am Your masterpiece in the making and I will enjoy the journey and honor You all along the way.

In Jesus' name,
Amen

Thirty-One

Present Your Case

Set forth your case, says the LORD;
bring your proofs, says the King of Jacob.

ISAIAH 41:21 RSV

The other day, I was in the customer service line at a store waiting to return something I had purchased. The woman in front of me was taking a really long time, and after a while I started watching more closely to see what was happening. She was standing there frantically searching through her purse, pulling papers out and getting more and more frustrated. One employee came over, then another. I could see that this woman was trying to return something, but she didn't have her receipt. She was doing everything she could to get her money back, but it was no use. She eventually packed up her things and walked out the door. When it was my turn, I went up to the counter with confidence, handed the clerk my receipt, and asked for a credit on my account. Everything went through just fine, and I received my refund without a problem.

If we look at this scenario on a spiritual level, there's a lot we can learn. The lady and I both wanted and needed the exact same thing, but the difference was she was pleading her case and I was presenting mine. She had no evidence to show that she had purchased that item from that particular store. She had no solid proof, and therefore, no entitlement to what she wanted based on the company's return policy. On the other hand, I had proof of my purchase. I was operating according to the guidelines set forth by that company. I presented my case with confidence, having my receipt in hand, and I received what I was expecting.

This is how we should approach God, with confidence. The Scripture tells us to come to God with boldness to receive His grace in our time of need. We should bring our proof, our evidence. We don't need to beg Him for anything. We don't need to plead with Him. He's already set up a "policy" in His Word for us to receive from Him. I received my refund because I knew I had my receipt. I was sure of where I stood with the store's policy.

Are you coming to God with confidence receiving what He has for you? Receiving His grace and mercy for your needs? Or are you struggling feeling like God is not listening and you are not worthy to receive His blessings? There is a great exchange that takes place when you come to God with confidence knowing you have His Word as proof of His blessing in your life.

If you've been busy pleading your case, if you've been

telling God how unfair things are or begging for things to change, switch today to presenting His Word to Him. It's easy to complain and say, "God, these people at work aren't treating me right. My back's hurting, and my child isn't doing right." All of those things may be true; however, don't just pray the problem, pray the promises. When you face difficulties, one of the best things you can do is find a promise in the Scripture and remind God of what He said. "God, You promised to restore health back to me, so thank You that healing is coming. You promised You would be my vindicator in my work. You promised that my children will be mighty in the land."

· ·

Let us then approach God's throne of grace with confidence, so that we may receive mercy and find grace to help us in our time of need.

—HEBREWS 4:16 NIV

· ·

I encourage you to come confidently to God every morning thanking Him for what He promised over your life: "Father, thank You that You promised that the path of the righteous gets brighter and brighter. You promised that You will withhold no good thing because I walk uprightly. You promised that You will do exceedingly and abundantly more than I can imagine." Then receive His grace and mercy. Don't leave empty-handed; there is an exchange that takes place, your need for His grace. When you start declaring God's promises and believing them, not only is faith going to rise in your heart, it's going to change your perspective. You won't go around with a victim mentality; you'll have a victor mentality. You'll be fearless when you know that God being for you is more powerful than the world when it's against you. You are worthy to bring your proof to God.

God is not obligated to bring to pass what we say, but He is obligated to bring to pass what He says. When you bring God the proof of His promises from His Word and believe in your heart that's when a great exchange takes place. God not only bends down to listen, He dispatches angels to go to work on your behalf. Forces of darkness are pushed back, chains are broken, favor is released in a new way, and impossible situations turn around.

. . . .

Heavenly Father,

Thank You so much that You are true to Your prom-
ises. Thank You that I can go boldly and confidently
before You and present my case with the proof of Your
Word. I am so grateful that I don't have to beg and
plead, but rather I can trust and rest that a great
exchange is taking place in my life. You're such a good
Father and I am so thankful to be Your child, worthy
of Your grace and mercy.

In Jesus' name,
Amen

Thirty-Two

• • • • • ● ● • • • •

The Blessing in Action

*Therefore by Him let us continually offer
the sacrifice of praise to God, that is, the fruit
of our lips, giving thanks to His name.
And do not forget to do good and to share,
for with such sacrifices God is pleased.*

HEBREWS 13:15–16 NKJV

The other day my son, Jonathan, went out of his way to make me feel extra special. I was so appreciative of his thoughtfulness. I called him and began to gush over his kindness. He replied, "Mom, I did that for you because I knew you'd appreciate it and I wanted to make you happy. Thanks for all you do for me." Jonathan not only articulated his gratitude with his words, but he had gone one step further when he expressed it with his actions. That got my attention and stirred my heart. It made me want to bless him in other ways. As his parent, his maturity moved my heart and it moved my hand of blessing toward him.

We show another level of maturity when we not only express our gratitude with our words, but with our actions as well. In the same way Jonathan got my attention, expressing gratitude to God through our actions gets His attention because it shows Him that He can trust us with His blessings. We need to not only thank God for what He has done for us, but to also thank Him with our actions. Let us bless others because we recognize the blessing on our own life.

When you do something for someone else—take them to a doctor's appointment, pick them up when their car is broken down, call them, cheer them up, or pray for them, God sees it all. Not only does your Heavenly Father take notice and keep record of your kindness toward His children, but He also pays back the blessing. When you go out of your way to help someone, you're saying with your actions, "God, thank You for making my day." The Bible says that when you refresh others, you will be refreshed yourself. In the same way, when you make someone else's day, God will make your day. When God sees you blessing others, He, in turn, blesses you. There are no blessings that compare with the blessings of Almighty God.

God spoke to Abraham in Genesis 12 and said, "I will bless you and you will be a blessing." It is God's nature and His heart to bless you so that you can extend the blessing to others. That Scripture infers that the two blessings are tied together. The blessing isn't supposed to stop with us; it is meant to perpetuate. When you recognize that you are blessed to be a blessing, it not only increases your value, but it gives you great purpose. God has already prearranged for you to do good works. Those good works will bring good things in your life.

God set a principle for generosity into motion, found in Luke 6:38, "Give and it will be given to you." If you're not using what God has given you to help others, your blessing is not going to continue in the way that it could and should. My son knew he was blessed, so he passed on the blessing. Are you passing on the blessings that God has given you? There is nothing closer to the heart of God than seeing His children doing something good for someone else and walking in the fullness of what they have been given.

* *

For if the willingness is there, the gift is acceptable according to what one has, not according to what one does not have.

—2 CORINTHIANS 8:12 NIV

* *

God is saying to you what He said to Abraham: "I have blessed you so you could be a blessing." Don't be afraid that you aren't able or don't have enough to make a difference, holding yourself back from blessing others. Recognize all of the blessings of God that are already in your life. You woke up to see another day. You have your health, a good job, and people in your life that love you and care about you. Don't go through life with a barely-get-by attitude. The Bible says that you should give from what you have, not from what you don't have. It's easy to think you don't have the time or the resources to be a blessing to someone because you may be looking at what you need. Turn it around. Instead of looking at your need, look at your blessings and live from a heart of abundance and thankfulness. God will not only show you how to bless others, but also new ways to receive His blessings into your life.

. . . .

Heavenly Father,

Thank You. I want to recognize that You have given me life today and I never want to take that for granted. I don't want to be selfish and only think of my needs, but I want to be aware of those around me. Your promises are true. I declare that I am blessed and I will be a blessing everywhere I go. I will have an abundance mentality, knowing I have everything I need to be good to people.

In Jesus' name,
Amen

Thirty-Three

Free from Offense

He who covers and *forgives an offense seeks love.*

PROVERBS 17:9 AMPC

For as long as we live we will have to guard ourselves from taking up offenses. Throughout our lives unfair things will happen. People will let us down; they will say things that hurt our feelings. And they may not always treat us the way we think they should. If we allow those offenses to take root in our heart they will cause us to become resentful and bitter.

I have witnessed some people who never let go of their bitterness over a divorce or the way someone treated them. And it has negatively affected their entire life. Bitterness and unforgivingness can weigh us down and take our peace.

- -

Overhearing *but ignoring what they said, Jesus said to the ruler of the synagogue, Do not be seized with alarm* and *struck with fear; only keep on believing.*

—MARK 5:36 AMPC

- -

Whatever someone said or did to hurt you, don't allow it to continue to hurt you by holding on to that offense. People can say what they want and they can act the way they want but no one can offend you without your permission. You have the right to ignore them. No one can make you take up an offense.

In these times I believe we have to get good at ignoring others' actions and opinions that could bait us into being offended. We can't allow the opinions of others to steal the joy, confidence, and freedom Jesus came to give us.

The Bible doesn't say offenses won't come our way, but it does tell us how to handle those offenses. The choice is ours: we can either dwell on what someone has done to us, tell other people about it, and let it keep us up at night; or we can push the offense out of our mind and heart and release it into the hands of God. He is big enough to take care of it.

Most of my life my family has been in the jewelry business so I grew up around gemstones and precious metals. However I find the story about pearls fascinating. Most people know that pearls come from oysters. The process an oyster goes through to make a pearl isn't easy. In fact, the oyster isn't trying to make a pearl. It is actually insulating itself from an irritant that gets into its shell to embed itself into the tender flesh of the mollusk.

The oyster secretes a lacquer-like substance called nacre, to protect itself from damage. As it works constantly, the nacre builds up and eventually seals off the irritant, and that is how a precious pearl is formed.

Offenses in our life can be just like the irritant in the life of an oyster. When someone mistreats us or says something hurtful, if we don't guard our heart, those offenses can do some serious damage and keep us from God's best. Like the oyster, if we refuse to allow that irritant to be embedded in our hearts, then God can make a beautiful pearl in our lives. The way we insulate ourselves from offense and keep our heart pure is to release the hurt to God. We push it out of our heart and put it into God's hands. Just like the oyster covers that irritant with nacre, so we must cover offenses with love in order to protect our heart from being damaged. This is not always easy, and it takes some work, but the result is worth it. What was meant to harm us can become a beautiful pearl of wisdom in our lives. How do we do that? We start by simply making the choice to forgive and declare God's Word over those offenses.

Scripture tells us to bless those who curse us and pray for those who spitefully use us. That's sometimes difficult.

But every time you declare, "I forgive the person who hurt me and I bless them in Jesus' name," it's like pushing that offense away from your heart and covering it with a beautiful layer of God's love. You must create a barrier between you and the offense.

What is in your heart will direct your life. I want to encourage you to be aware of what is trying to pollute your heart. Push out any offense and cover it with God's Word and prayer. And, instead of harming you, the offense will produce a beautiful pearl of God's love.

. . . .

Heavenly Father,
I make a decision today to push out the hurts and offenses that have been taking up room in my heart. I refuse to let anything that is not good for me to stay in my life. I know that when I let go of the pain, I am releasing myself into the freedom that You have for me. Help me to keep my heart free from offense as I look to You and Your love for my life.

In Jesus' name,
Amen

Thirty-Four

· · · · · ● ● ● · · · ·

Ask for Wisdom

But anyone who needs wisdom should ask God,
whose very nature is to give to everyone without
a second thought, without keeping score.
Wisdom will certainly be given to those who ask.

JAMES 1:5 CEV

All through life you face everyday decisions as well as major decisions—which school you'll go to, what vocation you'll pursue, who you'll marry, what house you'll buy, and how to save and spend your money. You may be standing at the threshold of a major decision today, wondering how you can resurrect your marriage, raise your children, or pay your bills. Our decisions affect all of those around us. We often struggle with the fear of making a wrong decision and its impact. Whether it's deciding to change jobs or a parenting choice, the weighty decisions you face can feel overwhelming.

The good news is God will give you the wisdom to help you make the right decisions. Even when you choose the wrong thing, He will never hold your mistakes against you but always offer you another way.

Consider young King Solomon, who took the throne when his father, King David, died. He was only nineteen or twenty years old at the time. His father had built up a great nation, and now the responsibility to rule the nation of Israel was all on the shoulders of Solomon.

One night God came to him in a dream. He asked Solomon what he wanted and promised it would be given. God's question in itself was quite the decision for Solomon.

You can imagine that he could have asked for anything—money, fame, or a long life—but young King Solomon asked for what he needed most of all: "God, what I need is Your wisdom to govern Your people and know right from wrong. I need an understanding heart to make the right decisions." God was so pleased with his answer that He not only gave Solomon wisdom, but He gave him power, influence, and great riches.

For the LORD gives wisdom; from his mouth come knowledge and understanding. He holds success in store for the upright.

—PROVERBS 2:6–7 NIV

I believe that's a powerful lesson to us today. We all need to ask for God's wisdom. Just as Solomon needed wisdom, we need wisdom. We are to "search for it as for hidden treasure." It's interesting that even though in our world today we have unlimited amounts of information available to us, what we really need is not more information, but the wisdom to discern the value of the information. You can have tons of information and even know God's Word, but if you can't apply it, it's not going to do you any good.

You don't have to have the answers to your financial struggles, your relationship issues, or even your kids' problems all by yourself. Where you struggle or fall short of answers is where God wants to be, and it's where you need Him most. God wants you to let Him help you find your solutions. Before you navigate the decisions that surround your challenges, first ask God for His wisdom. It's the single best decision you can make.

One of the best places to go for wisdom is the book of Proverbs, which was written by King Solomon. It's a book that's full of advice and life lessons, simple in its form, easy to digest, and easy to apply. That's what wisdom is. It's a simple revelation of God's wisdom that we can apply to our everyday lives. Ask for wisdom and read the book of Proverbs. Read it and reread it, over and over again. It is loaded with powerful nuggets of God's truth, which will impart His wisdom into your life.

. . . .

Heavenly Father,

I ask You for Your wisdom to make the best decisions for my life. Not just for the major decisions, but I seek Your wisdom for the choices I make every day. I want to walk in the counsel of Your word. Help me to apply wisdom and knowledge and to gain understanding in every aspect of my life. I am aware that my decisions affect all of those around me, so thank You for guiding me along the best path and leading me with Your wisdom to where I need to be.

In Jesus' name,
Amen

· · · · · · ● · · · · ·

Thirty-Five

Dedicate Your Actions to God

Commit your actions to the LORD,
and your plans will succeed.

PROVERBS 16:3 NLT

When my son, Jonathan, was a little boy I encouraged him to learn to play a musical instrument. I wanted him to have the experience of committing to something that would bring results and benefit him in the future. Jonathan decided he'd like to learn guitar, so we got him a guitar and he started lessons.

Everything tried to interrupt his lessons. Friends wanted to hang out. Plans kept coming up and it was never a good time to practice. But I encouraged him to stay dedicated. At times, Jonathan must have thought that I was being mean when other kids were outside playing and he was stuck inside practicing his guitar.

As a ten-year-old boy, he probably felt as if I was punishing him by having him stick to his commitment. Quite often commitment can feel like restriction, it can be hard and unpleasant at times. At any age or season in life, once you've made a commitment and set a goal to accomplish what is in your heart, you will always face obstacles that get in the way. We all have opportunities to give up on what we hope for, walk away from an uncomfortable situation, or slack off because things get difficult and we're afraid we might fail. If we are going to be our best and reach our dreams, we are going to have to stay committed.

We can't be half-in and half-out. We need to have a made-up mind that no matter what gets in our way we are not going to quit. You can't fail unless you quit. Let's be never give-up people. God wants to give us the strength, fearlessness, and resolve to keep our commitments.

Stay dedicated to your family, your jobs, your dreams, and your goal. Even when things don't feel like they are going your way, call out to God and don't give up. God is your source and He has the final say. God put inside you everything you need. Commitment brings out your potential. Your gifts and talents just need to be developed. You have the strength and courage to stay dedicated to your family. You have the determination to accomplish that goal of getting your health back. You have the wisdom to start that business, but it takes perseverance. Remember you are a "no lack" person because God made you that way.

Jonathan stayed at those guitar lessons even on the days he didn't feel like it. Even on the days it didn't look like he was accomplishing anything, Jonathan stuck with it. Eventually he began to see the reward of his commitment. The rewards are what give us the strength to see things through. Jonathan had to serve that commitment whether he felt like it or not, but then that commitment began to serve him. Once he began to see how that commitment was producing the results he had hoped they would, I never had to ask him to practice again. It became easier and he wanted to do it. He began to enjoy the fruit of his discipline and dedication.

None of us will ever experience all that is possible without commitment. Commitment is not just an intention, it is a plan in action. It takes discipline and determination, which may not always seem fun, but the reward is always beneficial. Don't give up; put God in your plans. He will see you through.

. . . .

Let us not become weary in doing good, for at the proper time we will reap a harvest if we do not give up.

—GALATIANS 6:9 NIV

. . . .

Do everything you can in your own power and God will do for you what you can't accomplish on your own. You just have to take that first step of faith.

Commitment is what leads to accomplishment. Remember, you will most enjoy what you've remained committed to. Choose to fully commit to the Lord, and dedicate your actions to the things that cause you to walk in freedom, confidence, and accomplishment. Do this by faith, and God will help you finish what you start.

. . . .

Heavenly Father,

Help me to understand the importance of commitment and to dedicate my plans to you. Give me the determination and strength I need to not give up. I believe, as I continue to serve my commitments, they will bring me joy, fulfillment, and a better understanding of the power that I have in You. I can do all things through Christ who strengthens me. And I will see my dreams and desires come to pass. Thank you for your commitment to me, Lord; I love you.

In Jesus' name,
Amen

Thirty-Six

· · · · · ● ● ● · · · · ·

Be God-Made

*God Who began the good work in you will keep
on working in you until the day Jesus Christ
comes again.*

PHILIPPIANS 1:6 NLV

The term *self-made* is often used to describe someone who became wealthy and influential all on their own. They are usually referred to as a self-made success because of their own determination and hard work. From YouTube sensations to app designers, these entrepreneurs get younger and younger all the time. I recently read an article detailing the journey of twelve young people who became millionaires before they were old enough to drive. That's impressive, isn't it?

But here's what that article didn't say. Whether you're twelve when you make your first million or forty-two when you invent a groundbreaking app, if those or other successes are achieved apart from God, they will ring hollow. Money, success, and the kind of joy the world offers can't be matched by what God can offer or the possibilities He has for you when you let Him shape your life. It's so much more fulfilling to be *God-made* than self-made. God wants to give us more than just what money can buy. He wants to give us success in our souls. He not only wants us to prosper financially but He wants our soul to prosper. The apostle Paul prayed, "I wish above all things that you would prosper and succeed even as your soul prospers." God wants us to be blessed so we can be a blessing on this earth. It's not by wealth, success, and influence that you become great, but by putting God in the center of your life and letting Him make you great. That's when your soul will prosper and you will live a life of blessing and fulfillment. When you are God-made, that's how you leave a legacy for people to follow.

. . . .

"I will make you into a great nation, and I will bless you; I will make your name great, and you will be a blessing."

—GENESIS 12:2 NIV

. . . .

The patriarch Abraham was a *God-made man*. Genesis 12 says that God asked Abraham to leave the comfort of his parents and where he grew up to follow Him to a new land. Obedient to God's calling, he was willing to pursue God, who would make him into someone great. Abraham's legacy wasn't built overnight. His journey took an enormous amount of faith and it had to be developed. Like you and me, he wasn't perfect. God is not looking for perfect people. You don't have to have it all together, but what you do need is a willing heart and a desire to follow God's plan for your life. He wants you to start today, just the way you are. He sees your greatness even if you don't.

But just like Abraham, you must be willing to trust God to work with you and help you become all you were created to be. No matter where you are on your journey, don't be discouraged. When self-doubt creeps into your mind and whispers, *God can't use me. I don't have the talent; I have made so many mistakes. It's too late*, take those thoughts captive and stop them in their tracks. If you want to erase a thought that is swirling in your head, you have to replace it. You have to think, *I am a work in progress. God is* making me *into who He is calling me to be.* And, when others seem to be doing better in life, or when you're tempted to take your own road instead of waiting for God to finish His work in you, remember that from those seasons of struggle your greatest transformation takes place.

God never abandoned Abraham, even when he tried to do things his own way and take his success of having a child with his wife into his own hands. Even when he made a mess out of things in his life, he never quit pursuing God to make him into who he was supposed to be. Abraham wasn't a failure when he took the wrong path; he was a learner because he never quit. *God made* Abraham not only to become successful in his wealth, but his family was blessed, and the world was changed forever. Abraham is known as the Father of Faith all because of his willingness to let God establish his potential, and because of his legacy; we can all stand in the blessing of Jesus Christ. That's a faith we can follow. Stay faithful to God and He will finish what He started in you. Don't settle for being self-made. Be *God-made* and watch your life unfold in ways you've only imagined. You will be more fulfilled and you, too, will be blessed, so that you can be a blessing and leave a legacy of faith.

. . . .

Heavenly Father,

Thank You that I am blessed in my life as I follow after You. I want to have faith like Abraham to keep going even when times get tough. I believe You are making a way for me even when I can't see it or feel it. You are the way maker and I trust You are always working in my life. I believe as I follow You I will take the best paths for my life and become the God-made person you have called me to be. I declare that I am blessed to be a blessing, and I will leave a legacy of faith for those around me.

In Jesus' name,
Amen

· · · · · ● ● ● · · · · ·

Thirty-Seven

Remind Him of His Word

*"Put me in remembrance:
let us argue together; put forth your case,
that you may be proved right."*

ISAIAH 43:26 ESV

Years ago, when my daughter Alexandra was younger, she came to me one day and said, "Mom, can I go over to my cousin's house now?" Well, I was a little preoccupied at that moment and preferred that she just stay at the house with me. So, without giving it a lot of thought, I said, "No; why don't you just stay here and play outside?"

But then she said something that really got my attention: "But Mom, you told me this morning that if I cleaned my room and fed the rabbit that I could go to my cousin's house this afternoon." She knew what I had promised, and she was holding on to that promise. She was boldly reminding me of the words I had spoken to her earlier that day.

- -

"Truly, I say to you, unless you turn and become like children, you will never enter the kingdom of heaven."

—MATTHEW 18:3 ESV

- -

The Bible says that we should have faith like a child. Even when it looked like Alexandra wasn't going to be able to go, she didn't back down. When I first said no, she didn't walk away sad and frustrated and give up on the promise; instead, she pressed in and spoke my very words back to me. She knew I loved her and she had the faith in me that I would be true to my word. When she reminded me of that promise I was faithful to it and took her to her cousin's house.

In the same way, when we bring the Word of God to Him, He is faithful to it. The scripture says in Isaiah 43:26, "Put Me in remembrance..." It's not that God forgets His Word. He already knows what He has said, but He wants to make sure that we have the faith and confidence to believe what He said, and hold to it. Don't get upset and frustrated and start complaining to God. Complaining only weakens your faith. Bring God's promise to Him, not your problem. Yes, we can talk to God about everything, but it is more effective when we find a promise that fits our need and build our prayer around it. If you need healing, Jeremiah 30:17 reminds us of God's promise that He will "restore you to health and heal you of your wounds." Take God's invitation today; come to Him with the confidence that He will keep His promises. Whatever your need is today, declare God's word and remind Him of His promises. It not only builds your faith, but God is faithful to His word and it sets the miracle you need into motion.

. . . .

Heavenly Father,

I don't come in my own words; I bring my need to You with the promise that Your Word will not return void, but it will accomplish what You desire and achieve the purpose for which You sent it. I believe that You are the same God today as You were with Abraham. You are the Lord, my provider. Thank You for the invitation to come boldly to You, that I may receive grace and mercy in my time of need.

In Jesus' name,
Amen

Thirty-Eight

Grow in Joy

*"I have told you this so that my joy may be
in you and that your joy may be complete."*

JOHN 15:11 NIV

His joy is *in* you. When you said "yes" to Jesus, nothing changed on the outside, but He gave you a new heart on the inside and filled you with His seeds of joy.

Joy is produced by putting your hope and trust in God; it is an attitude in your heart that is cultivated. As you make the choice to tap into the joy that He gives you, it changes the attitude of your heart.

I have a lemon tree that has produced so many lemons through the years. But when I first got it, there were no lemons on the tree at all. It looked like an ordinary tree with green leaves. The tag said it was a lemon tree but there was no visible fruit on it. I took the tree home and planted it in a sunny spot and in good soil. I watered it, fed it, and soon I began to see small flowers on the branches of that tree. It wasn't long after that I noticed small round fruit beginning to develop. As time went on those lemons began to show up as fruit on that tree. Even though I couldn't see the fruit at first, inside the DNA of that tree was the ability to produce big, beautiful lemons.

God has put His DNA on the inside of you and you have the ability to produce an abundance of joy. It may feel small, but when you cultivate it by putting it in an atmosphere of faith, praising God for all He has done and all He is going to do, you will see the fruit of joy become more apparent in your life.

Joy is your defense against the stress and strain that life throws your way. That is why Jesus prayed that you would produce joy and have it to the fullest. That means His joy is always there, even in the tough times. When everything seems to be coming against you, you can tap into joy by rejoicing in the God who is in control of the storm. Produce joy in your heart by trusting God for the turnaround. Anyone can get depressed, complain, and feel sorry for themselves, but that is not going to give you the strength you need to bring you out.

You may be in a difficult situation today and wondering if you will ever experience joy and happiness again. The key to staying strong in God is cultivating the joy that is in you.

When Nehemiah was encouraging the people in the rebuilding of the walls of Jerusalem, they were under extremely difficult circumstances. He said to the workers, "Go home and celebrate with a feast…for the joy of the Lord is your strength" (Nehemiah 8:10). Those were his instructions for them—to pause from the stress of the situation. Take time to celebrate in the presence of God.

He knew they needed to tap into the joy that would refresh them so that they could continue to move forward and complete the task.

That's what joy does. It gives us the strength of heart to move forward. It fuels our courage to keep going when things are difficult.

. . . .

Though you have not seen him, you love him; and even though you do not see him now, you believe in him and are filled with an inexpressible and glorious joy.

—1 PETER 1:8 NIV

. . . .

I love what the psalmist David prayed: "God, renew the joy of my salvation." David was saying, "God, I don't want to forget all that You have done for me. I want to recount Your goodness toward me and how You gave me victories in my past. You delivered me from Saul when he tried to kill me." He rejoiced in the God of his deliverance. David turned his negative thoughts around with positive affirmations of faith. He rejoiced and was grateful even when things weren't going his way.

Don't let the negativity of this world hold you back

by causing you to forget all the good things in your life. Be grateful and express it. Our gratitude should be verbal. We should get up every day rejoicing and celebrating the good in our life. We should thank God, thank people, and appreciate the good qualities in ourselves. Start a list of what you are thankful for. Verbalize it every day. You will find confidence and strength when you tap into the joy of being grateful; it will refresh your soul and give you the strength to carry on.

. . . .

Heavenly Father,

Thank You for putting inside me the joy that will make me strong and keep me moving forward in my faith. When life is trying to convince me that there is no hope, I won't be afraid, but I will keep my hope alive by cultivating joy through my gratitude. I will count my blessings every day. I know You love me and are helping me in every area of my life. Thank You for renewing my strength as I receive my joy that is found in You.

In Jesus' name,
Amen

· · · · · ■ ● ■ · · · ·

Thirty-Nine

Servant Leader

*"Just as the Son of Man did not come
to be served, but to serve, and to give his life
as a ransom for many."*

MATTHEW 20:28 NIV

Inside every human spirit is the desire to succeed and to achieve in life. It started when God told Adam in Genesis, "Be fruitful and multiply; fill the earth and subdue it; have dominion over every living animal." There is nothing wrong with position and influence as long as it doesn't go to our heads. Sometimes people seem to have it all but still find they want more. They are looking for fulfillment through their achievements. They are seeking greatness in all the wrong places. It's not always our success here on earth that makes us feel great. The fulfillment and greatness that God wants us to have comes through caring for and loving others. We should use the positions that God gives us to make a meaningful contribution to the people around us. Rather than any title or professional role, it's our *heart* position that makes life great.

I was at the birthday party of a seventy-five-year-old man who happens to be extremely wealthy. It was such a warm celebration and I was very taken by this man's engaging presence as he told me about his life, his biggest accomplishments, and what had meant the most to him: It wasn't the professional status or houses or boats or cars that he'd acquired, but the countless opportunities he had to use his position to help others. That is what he most valued in his life, using his gifts in service. This man's life reveals a valuable lesson to us all. No matter our financial means, you and I each have the capacity for greatness through service.

. . . .

Each of you should use whatever gift you have received to serve others, as faithful stewards of God's grace in its various forms.

—1 PETER 4:10 NIV

. . . .

It's hard sometimes to wrap our heads around servanthood as a great life. Our culture doesn't model service as the key to success, but rather success as being one who is served. What we see are people stepping over people, and doing things to try to gain more power and authority. However, Jesus gave us the ultimate example of greatness at the Last Supper as He sat with His disciples, overhearing them dispute among themselves who among them was the greatest, and speculating upon their status with Him. They could have been comparing their qualifications, or who was with Him most often when He performed

His miracles. As they competed among themselves, Jesus knew they hadn't yet grasped the concept of being great. Jesus did something profound that demonstrated to them what greatness was all about. He rose from the table and astonished the disciples as He prepared to wash their feet. By doing this, He showed them greatness through service and humility. His example of washing their feet spoke louder than any words that He could have said. Serving one another was not below their position and the authority they had been given; it was part of their position and authority. He wanted them to know that it was a privilege to serve others. Service is what makes us great. Jesus' concept of greatness is found in service. And through His loving kindness, He set the standard.

When I look back over my life, I want to be like my seventy-five-year-old friend, whose heartfelt passion was to use his position and influence to serve others with what God had entrusted to him. We can all use what we've been given to make a difference in the lives of others. Will we be the people who are on the lookout for those we can help? Just like Jesus stooped down to wash the disciples' feet, let's be people who use our time and influence to make others feel great. That's the life Jesus came to give us, a life of meaning and purpose. A life free from the burden of chasing worldly success.

No matter what position or title you hold on this earth, you can use your influence to serve others. You are called and equipped to be a great leader by being a great servant, which is who you can be from wherever you are right now.

. . . .

Heavenly Father,

Thank You that the true meaning of life and greatness is found in serving others. I want to be free not to be consumed by my own desire for achievements, but to find my greatness by looking for those to whom I can lend a helping hand. I want the position and favor that You have taught me, not the kind that would only serve myself. I want to bring healing and wholeness to others. Thank You for showing me what true greatness really is.

In Jesus' name,
Amen

Forty

· · · · · ● ● ● · · · ·

Stay Balanced

By the seventh day God had finished the work
he had been doing; so on the seventh day
he rested from all his work.

GENESIS 2:2 NIV

We live at such a great time in history. We can enjoy many more freedoms and take advantage of opportunities that weren't available in the past. Because of this, we also seem to wear more "hats" than ever before—employee, employer, mother, companion, friend, chef, counselor, housekeeper, and investor—and the list goes on. It's easy to get so wrapped up in all that we're doing that we don't take care of ourselves.

Most of us have been on an airplane and have heard the flight attendant give instructions about what to do in case of an emergency landing. They talk about the flotation devices, pathway lighting, and how to help the passengers beside you, and they explain how to use the oxygen mask that falls from above your head. They say something like, "Place the oxygen mask over your nose and mouth before assisting children or those around you." The most important part of assisting others in a situation like that is to make sure you are alert and strong, then you can help those around you. That makes sense in an emergency. But sometimes we forget the importance of how that plays out in everyday life, and how the situations in which we find ourselves affect those around us. If we're going to take care of anyone else properly, we need to first take care of ourselves.

God never planned for us to live stressed-out and overbooked. He created the world and all that is in it, and then even He took a day off. In doing so, He showed us the importance of striking a balance between busyness and rest. Like I heard someone say, "You have to *show up* for yourself before you can *show up* for others." Think about it—if you are empty, how will you have anything to give? If you are constantly giving and never replenishing, you will be left drained.

A hundred years ago, the main cause of illness was infection. Today, the main cause of illness is stress. When was the last time you took the day off or took some time to recharge your battery? Sometimes, you might feel guilty if you're not busy. But if you take on too much, you'll burn valuable energy and you won't have the stamina to be your best. If you're going to live fearlessly and free, you need balance in your life.

For God has bought you with a great price. So use every part of your body to give glory back to God because he owns it.

—1 CORINTHIANS 6:20 TLB

God wants you to find rest and peace in Him. All three parts of your being—physical, emotional, and spiritual—should be in sync for you to function most productively. Your body is the temple of God, and you must honor Him with the care you take of it. Seek balance, and try to be healthy and God-honoring in every part of life.

You are important not only to the people around you, but to God. Put yourself on your list of important things to tend to, even if that means scheduling thirty minutes of "me time" in your daily planner. Sometimes, just taking a walk in the park, looking at the birds, and some fresh air is enough to rejuvenate you. When I'm working in my home office, on a nice day I take a break and go outside. I breathe in and out slowly to bring a relaxed and balanced feeling to my mind and body. Whatever it is that refreshes and refocuses you will be a good investment of your time.

Investing in yourself also means investing in your personal growth. Maybe you need to join a gym to get healthy or invest in some online learning tools or leadership books. You might be surprised at how a few small deposits in yourself can pay off in a big way. I believe when you are doing the best you can to stay in good shape spiritually, physically, and mentally, you will see a difference in your family dynamics, jobs, and even your relationship with yourself. When you value yourself and prioritize self-care, you'll eliminate much of the stress you feel each day.

If you had an expensive family heirloom, you would take care of it. You wouldn't mistreat it, or let it get beaten up or worn down, because it is valuable. You are valuable, too, so take care of yourself.

. . . .

Heavenly Father,
Thank You for the life You have given me, the responsibility and family You have entrusted to me. I want to love and enjoy my life and be a good steward of it. Help me to recognize the importance of staying physically, spiritually, and emotionally strong. Help me to eat right, exercise, and always put Your word in my heart. Thank You for a balanced life and the freedom it brings.

In Jesus' name,
Amen

· · · · · ● ● ● · · · ·

Forty-One

Control Your Thinking

For as he thinks in his heart, so is he.

PROVERBS 23:7 AMPC

Our thoughts are a powerful force in our lives. They affect our attitude, outlook, and what we're able to accomplish. The Bible says in Proverbs that what we think in our heart is who we are. It's important to take control of our thoughts because they shape our character and what's possible for us. When we set our minds on God, our relationship with Him, and what is good, we become more like Him. We are freed from fear and negative thinking and are empowered to achieve our best.

Some researchers estimate that most humans have tens of thousands of thoughts each day, with over half of them being negative. Now that is a scary thought. Negative thinking is an attack on our ability to reach our potential and experience fulfillment. This starts with a single bad thought; if we allow that thought to take root, we give it control. That thought leads to a belief: *Our spouse doesn't value us. We'll never measure up. We're not going anywhere.* These are the thoughts that entrap us and hold us back. They are thoughts that originate from fear, and God hasn't given us a spirit of fear. Those thoughts aren't from God so they don't belong to you.

Thoughts that create a negative outlook, worries, and anxiety are not the thoughts of God. The Bible encourages us to turn that kind of thinking around by thinking thoughts that are excellent, noble, lovely, admirable, and praiseworthy. That is how we renew our mind and begin to see with a God perspective.

I recently talked with a friend whose husband was going through a hard time. He was a consultant in between jobs and was having a hard time finding the motivation and confidence he needed to pin down his next project. The months passed and she saw his happiness go downhill. She tried to help him discover prospects, but he kept finding the negative in them—either the pay was lacking or he didn't think the job matched his expertise.

The peace of God, which transcends all understanding, will guard your hearts and your minds in Christ Jesus.

—PHILIPPIANS 4:7 NIV

I encouraged her to help him shift his thoughts. He needed to recognize the good things in their life before he could see the possibilities ahead of him. The next time we spoke, she was ecstatic to share that her husband had begun to focus on the positives of each day. He now started each day thanking God for his health, and he tried to enjoy some extra quality time with his family while things were slow professionally. Once he got control of his thinking and regained his peace, sure enough, the job offers started to come in again.

You can take control of your thinking and experience the amazing things God can do in your life. Negative thoughts will always try to creep in, but you don't have to let them stay. Don't allow fear, frustration, or confusion to dwell in your mind and control your life. With a more positive outlook, life will begin to go your way. Instead of being controlled by your thoughts, start controlling them. Trust God to give you peace about the situations that make you anxious, and set your thoughts on where you want to go. When you send your mind in the right direction, you'll see miracles happen and the good things that are possible for you.

. . . .

Heavenly Father,
*I have felt the power of negative thoughts and have
seen the impact they can have in my life. I pray that*

You will empower me today to take control of my thoughts. I'm grateful to You for the blessings of this day, and I will focus my mind on what is positive in my life. I trust that Your hand is on my future and I give You my worries and concerns today knowing You have me in the palm of Your hand.

In Jesus' name,
Amen

Forty-Two

. . . . . ● ● ● . . . .

Be Committed
to Love

Above all, love each other deeply,
because love covers over a multitude of sins.

1 PETER 4:8 NIV

I was talking to a man who was celebrating his twenty-fifth wedding anniversary. It was fun because I could tell how much he loved his wife. He said something interesting to me. "You know, I love so many things about my wife, but there are moments when she's not so lovable. There are some things she does that don't make it so easy." Then he smiled and added, "But you know I love her anyway." I looked at him and said, "That's right, because you made a commitment to truly love her, and that's why you're where you are today."

We would all love to have great relationships. We want our marriage to be like that couple's. How wonderful to have such a great home life. But my friend's candid take on love gives a glimpse of what that kind of relationship requires. His commitment to a good marriage with his wife means having the self-control to keep his mouth closed in the times when she isn't so lovable, to let his love for her be greater than any wrong she could do him. It's so easy to say things that can jeopardize our commitment to love in tense moments when we feel wounded. But my friend chooses to focus on his wife's lovely qualities, the things that he adores about her, rather than the qualities that could disrupt their love. A few negative personality traits—and we all have them—should not diminish the commitment of our love.

- -

Love is patient, love is kind. It does not envy, it does not boast, it is not proud. It does not dishonor others, it is not self-seeking, it is not easily angered, it keeps no record of wrongs. Love does not delight in evil but rejoices with the truth. It always protects, always trusts, always hopes, always perseveres. Love never fails.

—1 CORINTHIANS 13:4–8 NIV

- -

The meaning, importance, and model of love is found all throughout the Bible. Love is not always easy, but it's always worth the commitment. Think of your sweet newborn baby when you first bring them home. They're so easy to love. Every moment with them in your arms feeds your soul. Then they start walking and talking and at first all they want to do is please you and to win your praise. As time passes and they become more motivated by their own desires, things change. That sweet baby is a teenager who talks back and pushes your buttons. But you love them through it. You know that God calls you to love them more than your own pride or need for respect. Sometimes it's a struggle to show godly love to others through the ups and downs of a relationship. But when we forget, God's Word offers the definition of true love as our guide.

In the book of Romans it says that even though we are sinners, Christ loved us enough to sacrifice himself for us. If you want good relationships, you're going to have to sacrifice—to be good to people when they're not being good to you. You have to learn to love fearlessly, to overlook offenses and to release anger and bitterness. That will take a great commitment but on the other side of that act of faith will be an amazing blessing. You'll be more fulfilled in your relationships than you could ever be without a godly approach to love. You'll look back over a lifetime and be glad you kept your commitment.

. . . .

Heavenly Father,
Thank You for Your sacrifice, and for the example of Your perfect love. You have empowered me to be

committed in my relationships, and to love fearlessly and freely. I also commit myself to You, Lord, and pray that You fill my heart with Your love, so that I can love others as You love me.

In Jesus' name,
Amen

Forty-Three

· · · · · ● · · · ·

God Can Exceed Your Expectations

*Now to Him who is able to do exceedingly
abundantly above all that we ask or think,
according to the power that works in us.*

EPHESIANS 3:20 NKJV

We think, *Ordinary*. God thinks, *Extraordinary*. We think, *Let me have enough to get by*. God thinks, *Abundance*. We think, *Let me manage this addiction*. God thinks, *Freedom*. We're asking for the possible when God wants to do the impossible. He specializes in exceeding our expectations, and what He has in store for us is bigger, more rewarding, and more fulfilling than we can imagine.

The apostle Paul said in Ephesians that God is able to do exceedingly abundantly above all we can ask or think. Paul wanted us to get it into our thinking that God's power can exceed our expectations. He can heal our bodies, open doors we can't open on our own, and protect us from accident and harm. God is always working in our life. He doesn't just do little stuff. He is the God of big miracles.

The Scripture tells of a man who had been crippled his whole life, and every day his family would carry him to the temple and set him outside by the gate. As people came in, he would ask them for money. He was forty years old and did this his whole life, day after day. He knew the routine. People would come in, he would beg for money, and here and there some coins would be thrown in his bag. This is how he survived.

One day, Peter and John came to the temple. The man went through his same speech, "Can you spare some change? Will you help me out?" Most people ignored him and kept walking, but Peter stopped and said to the man, "Look at us." The Scripture says the man looked up expecting to receive a gift. I can see him holding his bag out, thinking they were going to throw some coins in, but Peter said, "I don't have any silver or gold for you, but I have something better. In the name of Jesus, rise and walk." Peter took him by the hand, pulled him up, and he was instantly healed. He started walking. He was so excited, he took off running, leaping, and thanking God.

Notice, the man was expecting a few coins. He was expecting the ordinary—the same thing that had happened for the past forty years, but God showed up and exceeded his expectations. He didn't see it coming. He thought he would have to lie by that gate and beg the rest of his life, but one moment of favor, one exceeded expectation, changed his whole life.

I love the fact that to this crippled man—even though he had low expectations, and even though all he anticipated was a few coins—God didn't say, "Too bad. I had something much better, but you don't have enough faith. I was going to let you walk, but you're not expecting enough." God is so merciful. Even when we don't have the faith, even when we think we've reached our limits, God says, "That's okay. I'm going to give you a blessing and show you favor in spite of that."

. . . .

"...For truly, I say to you, if you have faith like a grain of mustard seed, you will say to this mountain, 'Move from here to there,' and it will move, and nothing will be impossible for you."

—MATTHEW 17:20 ESV

. . . .

The Scripture says when we have faith the size of a mustard seed, nothing is impossible. A mustard seed is one of the smallest seeds. God could have said, "If you have great faith, if you never doubt, and never get discouraged, then I'll do something big." But God knew there would be times that we didn't have the faith we thought we needed to reach our destinies. Instead He said, "If you have just a little bit of faith, that's all you need, then I'll show up and exceed your expectations."

That crippled man never dreamed he would be walking and running. After forty years of sitting at that gate, begging day after day, God showed up and did for him what he couldn't do for himself. God has some of these *more-than-you-can-ask-or-think* blessings in store for you. You may have been a certain way for a long time, and the situation seems like it will never change. The medical report doesn't look good. You don't have the education you need. You have gone as far as your present resources can take you. The good news is none of that stops our God. He controls the universe. One touch of His favor can turn any negative situation around.

Like Peter told the crippled man, it's your time to rise up and walk. It's your time to be free, it's your time to break bondages, it's your time to go to new levels, and I believe that every force that's holding you back is being broken right now. God is releasing healing, favor, opportunities, restoration, and freedom. This is a new day. God is doing a new thing. He's going to exceed your expectations. Get it into your thinking. There is nothing that is happening in your life that is too hard for our God.

. . . .

Heavenly Father,

Thank You that You are the God that does more than I can ask or think. You are not limited to my small faith, but Your Word says that You will move mountains and do the impossible with my mustard seed–size faith. I believe that You are always at work in my life and You will exceed my expectations as I look to You. My prayer is that I will see Your goodness come bursting forth in my life.

In Jesus' name,
Amen

Forty-Four

· · · · ● ● · · · ·

Your True Identity

*And he has identified us as his own
by placing the Holy Spirit in our hearts
as the first installment that guarantees
everything he has promised us.*

2 CORINTHIANS 1:22 NLT

I received a text message on my phone alerting me of a credit card transaction that had been used in my name. I was being alerted because I have theft protection on my credit card account. It recognized that this was not part of my normal usage pattern. The message requested that I reply "No" if this was not my charge and "Yes" if it was my charge. Upon further investigation, I discovered that my credit card was used at a gas station in another city, and then in an auto parts store in a small town nearby. There were additional charges using my credit card for miles down a Texas highway. Someone had stolen my credit card and was using my identity to make purchases that weren't mine. I had to cancel the card and get an entirely different card and account number.

I am so glad I have a safeguard against identity theft. According to identity fraud research, the number of consumers who fell victim to identity fraud was 14.4 million people in 2018. Identity theft is a problem for many businesses and people all over the United States and around the world.

Not only can we fall victim to identity theft in our finances, we can also fall victim to identity theft in our soul. There is a thief who wants to hijack our self-image and distort the way we see ourselves. We have an enemy of our soul who tries to use whatever he can to rob us of our identity in Christ, our passion and purpose, and ultimately stop us from fulfilling our God-given destiny. It's not only a good idea to protect our finances and personal information; we need a LifeLock protection plan over our souls. When we know the One who created us and have a personal relationship with Him, we can safeguard ourselves from the deceit of not seeing ourselves as God sees us.

As far back as the Garden of Eden, the enemy has been trying to steal what God intended for us. He wants to take our worth and value because he has none. That's what a thief does; they steal what they don't have.

. . . .

"The thief comes only to steal and kill and destroy; I have come that they may have life and have it to the full."

—JOHN 10:10 NIV

. . . .

However, God wants us to receive what He has done for us through His Son, Jesus, and for us to walk in the fullness of who we were created to be. Embracing your identity in Christ will shape your self-image and what you project to the world in an incredible way. Knowing who you are and Whose you are will help you uncover the purpose you were created for. Nothing will be able to stop you from accomplishing all that God has destined for you. It opens a world of new possibilities for what you can achieve. There is power when you know your true identity. You are a child of God, so you can come to God with confidence to receive from the heavenly account He has stored up for you. You have a right to healing, restoration, peace, and joy. Whatever you need you have as an inheritance because you are a Child of God; and you have a right to receive it. That's why the enemy works so hard to discourage us. He lies to try to convince us that we don't matter, that we aren't valuable, and that God could never use us.

You may have faced some ups and downs in your life or made some mistakes that you regret, but none of that changes your identity. You are His child, His masterpiece. You are made in His image. Jesus offers the grace to cover your mistakes. You can still live an abundant life free from regrets of the past. You are not a victim; you are a victor.

You are not overcome by life; you are an overcomer. Even if bad things have happened to you in life, those situations don't define you. Don't allow one season of your past to define your future. There is nothing the enemy would like more than for you to shrink back and wear labels that aren't yours to wear. He doesn't want you to understand your worth and value in God's eyes, so he will trick you into believing what happened to you is who you really are. Don't take the bait. It's time to reclaim your identity. It's time to take back your purpose and your passion.

"God identifies you as His very own." Let that sink into your spirit a moment—He has already identified you as His very own child. God knows who you are. But as great as that truth is, if *you* don't know who you are, you'll never fulfill your divine calling or walk in the freedom that's already yours. Don't allow the enemy to steal your identity. Start spending time looking into the mirror of God's Word so that you will reflect the image of God everywhere you go. Own who you are and let your true identity set you free to be confident and fearless as you honor God.

. . . .

Heavenly Father,

Thank You that I am found in You and I wear the identity of what you have done for me. You have made me Your child, and I want to walk in my authority, not allowing anything to steal what is rightfully mine. You have called me to come to You with great confidence knowing you have good things in store for me. I will shake off negative labels from my past and reclaim who I was meant to be. Thank You for the privilege to be Your child.

In Jesus' name,
Amen

· · · · · ● ● ● · · ·

Forty-Five

You Already Have What You Need

I will greatly rejoice in the Lord, my soul shall be joyful in my God; for He has clothed me with the garments of salvation, He has covered me with the robe of righteousness, as a bridegroom decks himself *with ornaments, and as a bride adorns* herself *with her jewels.*

ISAIAH 61:10 NKJV

I heard a story about a car that slid off a snowy country road in Pennsylvania and became lodged in a ditch. The driver couldn't get the car out by herself, so she asked for help from a nearby farmer and his faithful horse Abe. The farmer agreed to let Abe try and pull her tiny car out of the ditch, as long as the horse didn't become distressed. With that, the farmer hitched Abe to the small car and called out, "Now pull, Ike. Now pull, Henry. Now, pull Caleb," and finally, "Now pull, Abe." When Abe heard his name, he leapt forward and pulled the car out of the ditch. The woman was so grateful—but also a little puzzled. She asked the farmer, "Why did you call so many other names before Abe's?"

The farmer smiled at the lady and explained, "You see, Abe is blind and couldn't see there weren't any other horses around to help him accomplish the difficult task. He needed to think he had help before ever trying to do such a hard thing."

Oftentimes, we operate a little bit like Abe. We are looking for reinforcement before we even attempt to accomplish what God has called us to do. We call on others for help when God simply wants us to use the talents and the strength He has already placed inside of us. You see,

God hasn't left anything out. He's not holding anything back. He's given you the right gifts, the right personality, the right connections, and the right opportunities to make it through any situation and overcome any obstacle. Through our relationship with Christ, we have all of the freedom to rise to our potential and become who we were created to be. There is nothing or no one that can keep us from our destiny. The people in your life don't even have to believe you've got talent that is uniquely yours to share with the world. They don't have to believe it or support you in order for you to succeed.

* * *

[Joseph] said to them, "Listen to this dream I had: We were binding sheaves of grain out in the field when suddenly my sheaf rose and stood upright, while your sheaves gathered around mine and bowed down to it."

—GENESIS 37:6–7 NIV

* * *

Remember the story of Joseph in the book of Genesis? His father showed him favor by giving him a special, colorful robe to wear—a robe that represented his father's love and the fact that Joseph was set apart. You'll also recall Joseph's jealous brothers. Well, this robe only further angered them. Then Joseph revealed to his brothers his special gift, an ability to interpret dreams—dreams that predicted he'd one day rule. As you might imagine, Joseph's brothers weren't exactly thrilled about their little brother's "gift." They didn't believe in his calling. Worse than that, they despised him and tried to hold him back from his destiny. Because of their jealousy, they even considered killing Joseph before stripping him of his beautiful robe and selling him into slavery.

Joseph was on his own—except he still had God's favor. Even though his robe had been taken, his brothers could not take away the robe of righteousness that God had given him. They tried to strip him of who he was, but Joseph didn't allow it. He knew that his brothers could not stand in the way of his destiny.

You probably remember how the story ends, but even as a slave, Joseph excelled and stood out. He went on to serve in the home of Potiphar, a high official of Pharaoh, and God continued blessing Joseph. Even when temptation came and circumstances again tried to rob Joseph of his anointing, and he was put in prison because of a lie, he still would not let anyone strip him of his calling. Eventually, God used Joseph's gift of interpreting dreams to take him from the prison to the palace, where Pharaoh put him in charge over the land of Egypt. The dreams God had given Joseph years before came to pass in spite of his brothers and all of the circumstances that had come against him. The call inside of him was much greater than any attack he had faced. And guess what? It's the same for you. The call inside of you is so big—much bigger than any naysayer or negative situation.

A while back, I was praying with a woman who was very fearful of the future because she lived with a man who was struggling with alcoholism. He wasn't a bad man but he didn't support her like he should, and she worried about their welfare all the time. Everything was so unstable in her world, and she simply could not see how God could ever use her to accomplish anything. I looked at her and told her that she had allowed her situation to dictate her future. She'd taken her eyes off of God and taken off her crown of favor in the process. In her own mind, she had become "the wife of an alcoholic"—that was her only identity. She no longer saw herself as a Child of the Most High God. I told her exactly what I'm telling you today: "God has given you gifts and talents, and you are covered with the robe of Christ's righteousness. The world didn't give it to you, and the world can't take it away. You are equipped to do exactly what God has called you to do, and the plan He has for your life is an amazing one. You don't have to settle where you are; you can move forward in freedom, knowing that God has got you."

Like Abe, you may feel that the struggle is too great without some reinforcement. Like Joseph, you may feel all alone. But thank God, we don't go by feelings. We go by faith. Wake up the mighty faith warrior inside of you and live with expectancy. You may have to encourage yourself in the Lord by saying out loud, "I am a child of God. I have a great calling on my life. I have gifts and talents inside of me that nobody else has, and God is going to use me mightily."

. . . .

Heavenly Father,
Thank You for calling me and equipping me. Help me, Lord, to walk in my calling every day—no matter the naysayers or the negative circumstances. Help me to keep my eyes on You as I fearlessly walk into my

destiny, the destiny you put inside of me, and realize that I'm never alone. I don't go by feelings, Father, but I go by faith. I am excited to see all of the good things You have planned for me, and I'm encouraged to walk through every door You open. Thank You for my robe of righteousness and my crown of favor. I love You, God.

In Jesus' name,
Amen

Forty-Six

. . . . . ● ● . . . .

Keep Your Eye on the Ball

Let your eyes look straight ahead;
fix your gaze directly before you.
Give careful thought to the paths
for your feet and be steadfast
in all your ways.

PROVERBS 4:25–26 NIV

When our son, Jonathan, was a little boy of about four years old, I took him into the backyard to teach him how to hit a baseball. I placed him in a hitter's stance, positioned myself at the right pitching distance from him, and tossed him the ball. Jonathan swung the bat with all the might his little four-year-old frame could muster, and he completely missed the ball.

We set ourselves up again, he swung the bat, and again, he missed the ball. I really wanted him to hit the ball, so I had to get him to pay attention and focus on that ball. I picked up the ball and said, "Jonathan, I want you to look at this ball very carefully. I don't want you to take your eyes off of this ball. Don't look away, don't pay attention to the dog, tune out the birds for a minute, and just keep your eye on the ball."

He took his stance, I tossed him the ball, and he took a swing. This time, his bat made contact with the ball and off it went into the backyard. He was so excited, and I began to cheer, "Way to go, Jonathan." When he focused his attention on that one thing—the ball—that's when he nailed it.

The Scripture says to look away from all that distracts you. Do you ever find yourself trying to accomplish a task or a project at work, or you set a goal for yourself, but distractions seem to stop the progress? Never before have opportunities for distraction been so prevalent in the structure of our lives. Whether we go to the airport, to the mall, to restaurants, or even to Disneyland, it is not uncommon to see people looking at their phones. We have become so accustomed to dividing our time among so many things, that it can lessen our productivity. It can cause us to strike out when it comes to the important things in life.

I have noticed that the key ingredient among successful people is that they are so focused on their tasks and are intent upon avoiding unnecessary distractions. They are productive because of the quality of the attention they dedicate to what it is they are doing.

. . . .

Be very careful then, how you live—not as unwise but as wise.

—EPHESIANS 5:15 NIV

. . . .

I knew a very successful man that would not take phone calls between 9:00 a.m. and 1:00 p.m. every workday. He set aside that time to put his full attention on his project. He knew his attention was at its peek at that time of day, so he used his time wisely. When his employees did talk to him, they knew not to distract him with unnecessary detail. It's interesting because not only did he train himself to avoid distractions during those hours, but the people around him learned about being focused too.

Evaluate what is going on in your life to see if you need to focus your attention on what is essential. What is keeping you from hitting that ball out of the park? Maybe you need to re-evaluate your family priorities, your relationships, or take better care of your health. Don't let the everyday distractions keep you from accomplishing what is truly important in your life. When you give those things your undivided attention by looking beyond the distractions, you can better keep your eyes on the ball, and you will find yourself hitting a home run every time.

. . . .

Heavenly Father,
I want to stay focused on the important things in my life. I don't want to be divided in my heart and mind from the meaning and value in my life that brings

me joy and happiness. I ask You to help me see what is causing me to get off track. Help me to be mindful of those things that so easily capture my attention. I dedicate my mind to You and will focus on being a good steward of my time and attention. Thank You for empowering and helping me to look past temporary things that try to entangle me and distract my attention from the important people in my life and the goals I want to accomplish.

In Jesus' name,
Amen

Forty-Seven

· · · · · ● ● ● · · · ·

Live in Shalom

"Peace I leave with you; my peace I give you.
I do not give to you as the world gives.
Do not let your hearts be troubled
and do not be afraid."

JOHN 14:27 NIV

A few years ago, we did a Night of Hope in the Jeru- salem Theater. After the historic evening, we spent a couple of days seeing the biblical sites of the city. It was an amazing trip and probably my most favorite ever. Every time we greeted a Jewish person, they would say, "Shalom." When we departed, they would say, "Shalom." When we walked into our hotel, the bellman would say, "Shalom." We heard "shalom" all day long, coming and going, and I loved it. *Shalom* is the Hebrew word for *peace*; it was beautiful to give it and to receive it wherever I went.

After we came home, I was still so into shalom. The word just reminded me of the peaceful feeling in Jerusalem and the greetings we exchanged with the people there. I bought coasters that said, "Shalom." I filled my house with "Shalom." For at least six months, I said, "Shalom" to everyone. My kids were like, "Mom, all right already."

But why wouldn't I be into it? Who doesn't want to have peace and tranquility and live free from strife? Absolutely—if you ask me, the more shalom the better.

* *

Turn from evil and do good; seek peace and pursue it.

—PSALM 34:14 NIV

* *

The truth of the matter is, as long as we live on this earth, there will always be something trying to steal our peace. The Bible says that we are to seek peace and pursue it. That tells me that peace is very important. Peace is something we have to be intentional about. It's something that we have to seek, and it's something we have to maintain. Peace is not the absence of trouble, but it's the presence of God in any situation. When you seek God, you are seeking peace.

You don't have to go all the way to Jerusalem—although I highly recommend it—to find peace. Peace is available to you right where you are today, because Jesus is with you where you are today. Jesus came so that you can have peace, no matter what you're going through. Whatever your worry is today, know that God is with you and you don't have to be afraid. Soak in His loving presence and allow it to bring you hope and calm. You can face anything with the peace of Christ in your heart. Shalom.

. . . .

Heavenly Father,
Thank You for coming alongside me as I face my troubles today. When pressure, worry, or anxiety try

to creep in and take my peace, I will look to You to help me overcome. I can always bask in the goodness of Your presence. It will comfort me and sustain me as You lead me to more peaceful days beside You.

In Jesus' name,

Amen

Acknowledgments

· · · · · · ● ● ● · · · ·

I have discovered that most accomplishments borne through discipline, patience, and diligent effort are the most satisfying of all. The effort we put into everything we do in our life should be as rewarding as the result. I was blessed to work with so many excellent people; it has been a joyful endeavor and a rewarding one. To all of them I owe my appreciation and gratitude.

First, I want to thank everyone at FaithWords/Hachette who brought their exceptional talents to this book, especially Daisy Blackwell Hutton and Karin Mathis.

I also want to thank my literary agents Shannon Marven and Jan Miller. Also, Rebecca Silensky and the exceptional team at Dupree Miller for their friendship, loyalty, and for the dedication to see each project through with excellence.

I would like to thank Virginia Bhashkar for her insight on this journey.

I extend a special thank-you to Joe Gonzalez for the cover design.

My warmest gratitude to my Lakewood Church family and our extraordinary staff. Together we are accomplishing the most important mission of all: sharing the love and hope of our Savior with the world.

I am grateful to have grown up in the family God gave to me. My mother, Georgine, and my father, Donald, who love me dearly. I'm grateful for the steadfast support and wisdom of my brother, Donald Jr. I am blessed to have a brother like him.

I cannot sufficiently convey the love and gratitude in my heart for how wonderful my husband and children have made my life. My husband, Joel, is my best friend, and the person who encourages me the most to achieve all that God has planned for me. And I cherish the love he has always shown me. When God gave to me my children, Jonathan and Alexandra, He did more than I could ask, think, or imagine. They fill my life with joy, laughter, and love, and they make me proud to be their mom every day.

Finally, and most important, I want to give my eternal gratitude and praise to my Lord and Savior, Jesus Christ. I dedicate this work to Him, because words are only words until He breathes His life into them.

About the Author

· · · · ● ● ● · · · ·

VICTORIA OSTEEN is a *New York Times* bestselling author, the host of a national radio program on Sirius XM, and the co-pastor of America's largest church, Lakewood Church, in Houston, Texas. She lives with her husband, Joel, and their two children in Houston, Texas.

We Want to Hear from You!

Each week, we close our international television broadcast by giving the audience an opportunity to make Jesus the Lord of their lives. I'd like to extend that same opportunity to you.

Are you at peace with God? A void exists in every person's heart that only God can fill. I'm not talking about joining a church or finding religion. I'm talking about finding life and peace and happiness. Would you pray with me today? Just say, "Lord Jesus, I repent of my sins. I ask You to come into my heart. I make You my Lord and Savior."

If you prayed that simple prayer, I believe you have been "born again." I encourage you to attend a good Bible-based church and keep God in first place in your life. For free information on how you can grow stronger in your spiritual life, please feel free to contact us.

Joel and I love you, and we'll be praying for you. We're believing for God's best for you, that you will see your dreams come to pass. We'd love to hear from you!

To contact us, write to:

Joel and Victoria Osteen

P.O. Box 4271

Houston, TX 77210

Or you can reach us online at
www.JoelOsteen.com.